The Egg, Dairy & Nut FREE Cookbook

by Donna Beckwith

www.donnaquest.com

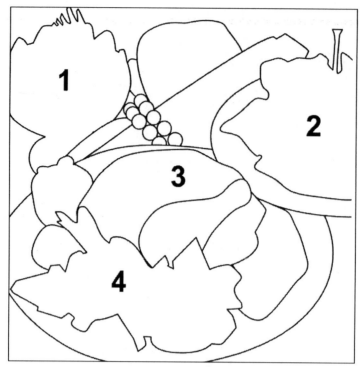

1. strawberry trifle, page 65
2. green salad with raspberry vinaigrette, page 143
3. Cornish hens with wild rice, page 117
4. assorted steamed vegetables

The Egg, Dairy and Nut Free Cookbook © Copyright 2004 Donna Beckwith.

All rights reserved worldwide. No part of this book may be reproduced or transmitted in any form by any means, electronic or mechanical, including photocopying, recording, or by any information storage and retrieval system, without written permission in advance from the publisher. Brief portions of this book may be reproduced for review purposes, provided credit is given to the source. Reviewers are invited to contact the publisher for additional information.

First Printing November 2004
Includes Index

ISBN 1-4120-3873-1

Front cover photo Darkhorse Studio • Author photo Milton B Taylor /
Imagery Cover and interior design by Cheryl McDougall / St Solo Computer Graphics Inc.

TRAFFORD
PUBLISHING

Published by
Trafford Publishing *on demand publishing service*™
Suite 6E–2333 Government Street
Victoria, BC V8T 4P4 CANADA
Phone 250 383 6864 (Toll-Free 1 888 232 4444) Fax 250 383 6804
Email to orders@trafford.com Web site: www.trafford.com
A DIVISION OF TRAFFORD HOLDINGS LTD

Trafford Catalogue number: 04-1681 www.trafford.com/robots/04-1681.html

10 9 8 7 6 5 4

Table of Contents

Introduction *4*

Acknowledgements *5*

Dedication *7*

Tips on how to alter recipes successfully *8*

Breads *9*

Cakes *23*

Cookies *31*

Desserts, Pies & Crisps *47*

Icing & Frostings *67*

Candy & Special Sweet Treats *75*

Main: Beef *89*

            Pork *102*

            Chicken/Poultry *108*

Soups *119*

Salads & Sauces *127*

Muffins *145*

Extras: Managing food allergies *157*

            Alternative names to look for in labels *162*

            Resources/associations to help you *163*

            Measurement tables *164*

Index of recipes *166*

This book or any part of it is not meant to replace professional advice. The author disclaims responsibility for liability due to using any information in this book.

Introduction

We were new parents! Aaron was happy, healthy and exclusively breastfed, but a persistent diaper rash had us very concerned. We tried everything, from creams for yeast infection to different diapers; nothing helped. One day during lunch my husband said, "Do you think it is something you are eating and passing on through the breast milk? We have not had any milk in the house for a couple of days and his rash has all but cleared up." So began our journey.

The information about food allergies and breastfeeding was very limited in 1993. Some doctors did not even believe there was a connection. Nevertheless, we began the process of eliminating milk and other foods from my diet. I kept a detailed food diary and journal of Aaron's skin condition. Throughout the next nine months the foods I isolated in addition to milk were wheat, peanuts and nuts.

When Aaron was eleven months old, an allergist confirmed his allergies to egg, milk, soy, peanuts and nuts. We had not singled out egg, but I had avoided most egg protein by eliminating baked wheat products. The allergist recommended that we always carry adrenaline: the fact that he did react to allergens passed on in breast milk indicated he was highly allergic.

Aaron outgrew his soy allergy when he was 5 years old, which allowed him more freedom in food choices. To date (2004), while Aaron remains allergic to milk, eggs and peanuts, he is growing up independent and confident in managing his allergies. Our second child Avril, born in 1995, arrived full term and healthy. As a precaution, during my pregnancy and while I breastfed her I avoided the foods Aaron was allergic to. Although we introduced these foods to Avril when she was older, and although she has tested negative for all food allergies, none of these foods have become part of her diet on a regular basis. Avril is well-educated about her brother's allergies, and she is very understanding and supportive.

This cookbook is the culmination of the past eleven years of cooking without milk, eggs, peanuts and nuts. We have learned through sheer determination, research, self-education and the support of those close to us. Cooking to accommodate these allergies is a challenge, but we have proven that with a liberal sprinkling of creativity, preparing great food for any occasion can be done. Our journey continues, as we work hard to create and maintain a safe and positive environment.

Have fun, and enjoy preparing delicious recipes.

Donna

Acknowledgements

Many family members and friends urged me to share with others what we have learned over the past 11 years. I am grateful for your encouragement.

To family and friends, our heartfelt thank you for your support in adapting recipes and lifestyles to include us in everything.

Thank you to all the restaurant staff who have accommodated us over the years. This has allowed us to enjoy the fun of eating out.

Thank you to Marilyn St. Marie, Cheryl McDougall and all the staff at St Solo Computer Graphics Inc. for their excitement, interest and above all their patience in this project. A special thanks to Cheryl for the all the layout work and the cover design.

Thank you to Jim Weseen for editing and proofing, as well as all the positive feedback and suggestions.

Thank you to Darkhorse Studio and to Chef Lee Helman from Truffles Bistro for the beautiful cover photo.

Aaron's quote:
I should get 10% of all profit from the cookbook, after all
there would be no cookbook without me!!

Avril's drawings are featured on these two pages.

The Egg, Dairy & Nut FREE cookbook *by Donna Beckwith*

Dedication

To Aaron, Avril and Doug:
We make a terrific team. I love you.

To Mom and Dad - the love and knowledge you patiently gave over the years has enabled me to create recipes and traditions for our family.

Love, Donna

Tips for cooking successfully without eggs and milk

Note – recipes include eggs for those who are not allergic and replacements for those who are.

1) Dairy free milk replacements are: Tayo® a fortified potato beverage, soy milk and rice milk. These products work well when modifying recipes. Individual taste will determine which product to use. A selection can be found in grocery stores as well as health food stores.

2) Do not over beat any recipe that does not include eggs, as it can become quite gummy.

3) Applesauce or milk replacement can be used to replace eggs. I use milk replacement if I do not want any apple taste in the recipe.

4) In some recipes whole wheat flour is often more forgiving, especially if you are not using an egg—for example in a bran muffin recipe.

5) You can increase the vanilla or use flavoured milk replacement in recipes if you require the additional flavour—for example in icings or some desserts.

6) Use plain or unflavoured milk replacement in all soups and main dishes.

7) <u>Lactose free does not mean milk-free</u>—always check ingredients, as milk proteins may be present.

chapter 1

Breads

Breads

White Bread   350°

1/2 cup	warm water	125 mL
1 tsp	sugar	5 mL
1 pkg (tbsp)	yeast	15 mL
2 cups	warm water (or milk replacement)	500 mL
3 tbsp	oil	45 mL
3 tbsp	sugar	45 mL
2 tsp	salt	10 mL
5 1/2–6 1/2 cups	flour	1.375–1.625 L

Dissolve sugar in 1/2 cup warm water, add yeast, and set aside.

Mix 2 cups warm water, oil, sugar and salt. Stir in set yeast and begin adding flour until dough is no longer sticky. Knead for 8 minutes. Put in greased bowl to rise for 1 hour. Knead 1–2 minutes and make into loaves and set to rise for 1 hour.

Bake at 350°F (180°C) for approximately 35 minutes.

Breads

Whole Wheat bread 350°

1 1/2 cups	warm water	375 mL
4 tsp	sugar	20 mL
4 tbsp	yeast	60 mL
4 cups	warm water (or milk replacement)	1 L
2/3 cup	molasses (optional)	150 mL
2/3 cup	oil	150 mL
3/4 cup	sugar or honey	175 mL
4 tsp	salt	20 mL
	ground flax (optional)	
6 cups	whole wheat flour	1.5 L
6 cups	white flour	1.5 L

* if using all whole wheat flour increase yeast by 1–2 tablespoons.

Dissolve sugar in 1 1/2 cup of warm water, add yeast and set aside for 10–15 minutes. Mix together warm liquids, oil, sugar and salt. Stir in yeast and begin to add flour. Knead for 8 minutes. This dough is stickier than white. Put in greased bowl to rise for 1 hour, knead again for 1–2 minutes. Put into pans to rise again for 1 hour.

Bake at 350°F (180°C) for approximately 35 minutes.

Breads

Oatmeal Bread 350°

1 cup	bran	250 mL
1 cup	old fashioned oats	250 mL
2 tsp	salt	10 mL
1/4 cup	molasses	50 mL
2 tbsp	brown sugar	30 mL
1/4 cup	oil	50 mL
2 1/2 cups	boiling water	625 mL
2 tbsp	yeast	30 mL
1 tsp	sugar	5 mL
1/4 cup	warm water	50 mL
6–7 cups	flour	1.5–1.75 L

Soak oatmeal and bran in the boiling water. Set yeast for 10–15 minutes. Combine liquids, add yeast and soaked mixture. Slowly add flour. Knead for 8 minutes and set to rise for 1–1 1/2 hours. Knead again, form into loaves and let rise for another hour. Bake at 350°F (180°C) for approximately 30 minutes.

Garlic Bread Broil

white or brown fresh bread or buns
- free of allergens
milk-free margarine
fresh garlic or garlic powder
parsley

Mix garlic and parsley into margarine and let sit for 1/2 hour—optional. Spread on bread and toast.

Breads

Biscuits - Grandma's 450°

2 1/2 tsp	baking powder	12 mL
2 cups	flour	500 mL
1/2 tsp	salt	2 mL
5 tbsp	shortening - milk-free margarine	75 mL
1 cup	milk replacement	250 mL

Cut shortening into dry ingredients, slowly add milk replacement. Roll onto floured surface and cut into shapes 3/4 inch (2 cm) thick. Bake at 450°F (230°C) for 10–15 minutes.

Bannock 425°

4 cups	flour	1 L
1 tsp	salt	5 mL
1/2 cup	lard/shortening/milk-free margarine	125 mL
1 tbsp	baking powder	15 mL
1 cup	warm water (may require a little more)	250 mL

Combine dry ingredients. Cut in lard until it resembles fine crumbs. Gradually add water to form a ball. Flatten to a thickness of about 1 inch (2.5 cm). Place on ungreased baking sheet. Bake at 425°F (220°C) for 25–35 minutes. Cool and cut into squares. Serve with jelly or jam.

Breads

Lefse

4 cups	mashed potatoes	1 L
	(mash hot and cool overnight)	
1/2 tsp	salt	2 mL
2 tbsp	milk-free margarine or oil	30 mL
1 cup	flour	250 mL

Mix together. Keep dough cool and take only what you will be using at one time. Make into small balls and roll lightly to make thin circles. Lift off of floured cupboard and dry fry.

French Toast

1 bag	thick sliced white bread (milk-free)	
2 cups	milk replacement (not fat free)	500 mL
2 tsp	vanilla	10 mL
2 tbsp	oil	30 mL
1/4 cup	sugar (white or brown)	50 mL

Stir together milk replacement, vanilla, oil and sugar. Dip bread on each side and fry at 350°F (180°C) on electric griddle or non-stick frying pan for approximately 3–4 minutes per side. Serve warm.

* Do not soak bread, lightly moisten each side.

Optional - sprinkle with icing sugar or cinnamon. They are good warmed up in the toaster the next day. The toast can be frozen and toasted at a later date.

Breads

Oatcakes 375°

3 cups	oats	750 mL
3 cups	white flour	750 mL
1/2–3/4 cup	white sugar	125–175 mL
1/2 tsp	salt	2 mL
2 tsp	baking powder	10 mL
1 1/2 cups	milk-free margarine	375 mL
	water to moisten dough	

Combine ingredients. Work in margarine as if for pastry. Moisten with water. Roll thin on floured/oat cupboard. Cut into squares. Bake at 375°F (190°C) for 15 minutes

Scones 350°

1 cup	milk-free margarine	250 mL
1 cup	milk replacement	250 mL
1 cup	sugar	250 mL
1/4 cup	milk replacement, applesauce (or 1 egg)	50 mL
3 cups	flour	750 mL
2 tsp	baking powder	10 mL
1 cup	raisins (optional)	250 mL

Cream margarine, sugar, applesauce (or egg) Add dry ingredients alternately with liquid—do not beat. Roll out on floured surface. Cut out and bake at 350°F (180°C) for approximately 15–20 minutes.

Breads

Blueberry Oatmeal Bread 325°

2 cups	white or whole wheat flour	500 mL
1 cup	oatmeal	250 mL
3/4 cup	sugar	175 mL
2 tsp	baking powder	10 mL
1/2 tsp	baking soda	2 mL
1/2 tsp	salt	2 mL
1 1/4 cup	milk replacement	310 mL
1/3 cup	oil	75 mL
2 tsp	vanilla	10 mL
1 tsp	grated lemon peel (optional)	5 mL
3/4 cup	applesauce milk replacement (or 2 eggs beaten)	175 mL
1 cup	frozen blueberries - do not thaw	250 mL

Grease 9x5 inch (22x12.5 cm) loaf pan. Combine all dry ingredients. Stir in liquids, add blueberries last and fold in gently. Bake at 325°F (160°C) for 50–60 minutes. Cool and remove from pan. Store in refrigerator or freezer.

Breads

Scottish Oat Scones   425°

1 1/2 cups	flour	375 mL
2 cups	rolled oats	500 mL
1/4 cup	white sugar	50 mL
4 tsp	baking powder	20 mL
1/2 tsp	salt	2 mL
1/2 cup	currants or raisins (optional)	125 mL
1/4 cup	applesauce or milk replacement (or 1 egg beaten)	50 mL
1/2 cup	melted milk-free margarine	125 mL
1/3 cup	milk replacement	

Combine first 6 ingredients together. Make well in center. Mix margarine and milk replacement. Pour into well. Stir to make soft dough. Roll and cut into shapes. Bake at 425°F (220°C) for 15 minutes or until risen and brown. Split and butter. Serve with jam or honey.

Soda Bread   450°

4 cups	flour	1 L
1/4 cup	sugar	50 mL
2 tsp	baking soda	10 mL
2 tsp	crème of tartar	10 mL
1 tsp	salt	5 mL
1 1/2 cup	milk replacement	375 mL

Mix dry ingredients together and make a well in center. Add milk replacement to make a soft dough. Mixture should not be wet, knead lightly on floured board. Shape into 7 inch (18 cm) round and place on baking sheet. With a knife make a deep cross over top. Bake at 450°F (230°C) for about 30 minutes—should sound hollow when tapped on. Wrap in damp cloth to cool.

Breads

Tea Biscuits   350°

2 cups	flour	500 mL
4 tsp	baking powder	20 mL
2 tsp	sugar	10 mL
1/2 tsp	crème of tartar	2 mL
1/2 tsp	salt	2 mL
1/2 cup	milk-free margarine	125 mL
2/3 cup	milk replacement	150 mL

Mix dry ingredients. Cut in margarine until very fine. Add milk replacement and stir with fork until mixed. Knead quickly about 20 times. Pat or roll to 3/4 inch (2 cm) thickness, cut into shapes and place on cookie sheet. Bake at 350°F (180°C) for approximately 15 minutes.

For crusty biscuits place 3/4 inches (2 cm) apart on baking sheet.

For soft sided biscuits place close together in shallow pan.

Breads

Quick Cinnamon Rolls 425°

2 cups	flour	500 mL
3 tsp	baking powder	15 mL
1 tsp	salt	5 mL
6 tbsp	milk-free margarine or shortening	90 mL
2/3 cup	milk replacement	150 mL
2 tbsp	soft margarine	30 mL
1/4 cup	white or brown sugar	50 mL
2–3 tsp	cinnamon	10–15 mL
	raisins (optional)	

Mix dry ingredients, cut in shortening until fine. Stir in milk replacement. Knead lightly on floured surface. Roll out to 1/4 inch (0.5 cm) thickness. Spread with softened margarine and sprinkle with sugar and cinnamon (and raisins). Roll up tightly like a jellyroll. Cut into 1 inch (2.5 cm) slices. Place in greased pan. Bake at 425°F (220°C) until done.

Frozen bread dough can also be used. Thaw and roll out, spread with margarine and sugar, roll and cut. Set to rise and bake.

Breads

Pancakes/waffles

1 cup	flour*	250 mL
4 tbsp	sugar	60 mL
2 tbsp	baking powder	30 mL
1/2 tsp	salt	2 mL
1/4 cup	applesauce, milk replacement (or 1 beaten egg)	50 mL
1 cup	milk replacement	250 mL
2 tbsp	oil	30 mL
1 tsp	vanilla	5 mL
	fruit can be added for a variation	

*can use 1/2 whole wheat flour and 1/2 white flour

Mix dry ingredients. Combine applesauce, (or egg) milk replacement and oil. Add to dry ingredients. Mix until smooth. Fry on nonstick pancake griddle. Serve with whipped topping and fruit.

** Some prepared mixes are also free of milk and egg products. Read carefully and keep on hand as they are very good.

Doughnuts

Use white bread recipe.

After first rising, roll out dough 1/4–1/2 inch (0.5–1.25 cm) thickness and cut into doughnuts. Let rise for a short time and deep fry. Roll in white sugar or spread with icing.

* Do not sugar or ice doughnuts that are to be stored or frozen as this changes the texture.

** Frozen dough can also be used for these. Unthaw, roll and cut out. Follow above directions.

Breads

Flour Tortillas

4 cups	whole wheat flour*	1 L
1 tsp	salt	5 mL
1/4 tsp	baking powder	1 mL
1/4–1/2 cup	oil or melted milk-free margarine	50–125 mL
1 cup	warm water	250 mL

*can use 1/2 whole wheat flour and 1/2 white flour

Mix dry ingredients. Rub in oil or melted margarine. Add water to make soft pliable dough. Knead briefly. Divide dough into 12–16 balls, cover and let rest for 20 minutes. Flour all and roll into thin circles between sheets of wax paper. Flour as needed to prevent sticking. Bake on an ungreased heavy skillet until brown specks appear on cooking side. Store in refrigerator or freezer. Fill with a favourite taco filling.

Cornbread   350°

2 cups	cornmeal	500 mL
1 3/4 cups	whole wheat flour	425 mL
1 1/4 cups	wheat germ - toasted	210 mL
1/2 cup	white sugar	125 mL
1 3/4 tsp	salt	8 mL
1 tsp	baking soda	5 mL
2 cups	milk replacement	500 mL
1/2 cup	oil	125 mL
1/2 cup	applesauce (or 2 eggs)	125 mL

Mix first 6 ingredients together then add liquids. Stir together—do not over-stir. Mixture can be poured into loaf pans and baked at 350°F (180°C) for approximately 1 1/2 hours or put into muffin cups and bake for approximately 15–20 minutes

These are very good served warm with honey.

Breads

Milk-Free Biscuits   450°

2 1/4 cup	flour	550 mL
4 tsp	baking powder	20 mL
1 tsp	salt	5 mL
1/2 cup	shortening	125 mL
1 cup	7-Up or Sprite	250 mL

Blend with pastry blender shortening, flour and baking powder. Stir in pop and mix lightly to make soft dough. Knead gently 8–12 times.

Roll and cut out. Bake at 450°F (230°C) for 12–15 minutes.

Filling for Cinnamon buns

1) Equal parts milk-free margarine and brown sugar, mixed well and spread on dough. Sprinkle with cinnamon, roll up and cut.

   or

2) Spread milk-free margarine on dough and sprinkle liberally with white sugar and cinnamon, roll up and cut.

chapter 2

Cakes

Cakes

Chocolate Cake 350°

3 cups	flour	750 mL
2 cups	sugar	500 mL
1/3 cup	cocoa	75 mL
2 tsp	baking soda	10 mL
1 tsp	salt	5 mL
3/4 cup	oil	175 mL
2 tsp	vinegar	10 mL
1 tsp	vanilla	5 mL
2 cups	water or milk replacement	500 mL
1/2 cup	applesauce (optional)	125 mL

Mix dry ingredients, make a well and add liquids. Stir, do not beat, until blended well. Make into cake or cupcakes. Bake at 350°F (180°C) for 25 minutes for a cake, less if making cupcakes.

Rice Crispy Cake

1/4 cup	milk-free margarine	60 mL
40	regular marshmallows	40
6 cups	rice crispy cereal	1.5 L
2 tsp	cocoa (can be added to the marshmallow mixture for a chocolate version)	10 mL
1 tsp	vanilla	5 mL

Melt margarine in large saucepan over low heat, add marshmallows and stir until melted, add vanilla. Pour over rice crispy cereal and stir until coated. Press into a greased pan. Can be eaten immediately or covered for later. This cake can be frozen. The mixture can also be formed into balls or pressed into small moulds for different shapes.

Cakes

Puffed Wheat Cake

1/3 cup	milk-free margarine	75 mL
1/2 cup	syrup	125 mL
1 cup	brown sugar	250 mL
2–3 tbsp	cocoa	30–45 mL
1 tsp	vanilla	5 mL
8 cups	puffed wheat cereal	2 L

Melt margarine in saucepan; add syrup, sugar, cocoa and vanilla. Bring this mixture to a boil for 1 minute. Remove and pour over puffed wheat cereal. Mix well and press into a greased pan. When cooled, slice into squares.

Graham Wafer Cake

	graham wafers	
1 cup	brown sugar	250 mL
1/2 cup	milk replacement	125 mL
1/2 cup	milk-free margarine	125 mL
1 cup	coconut	250 mL
1 cup	graham wafer crumbs	250 mL

Line bottom of pan with whole graham wafers. Boil brown sugar, milk replacement and milk-free margarine for approximately 4 minutes, add coconut and crumbs. Mix well and spread on whole wafers in pan. Cover with whole wafers. Press gently into pan and ice with your favourite icing.

Cakes

White Cake   350°

2/3 cup	milk-free margarine	150 mL
1 3/4 cup	sugar	425 mL
1 1/2 tsp	vanilla	7 mL
2 3/4 cups	flour	675 mL
2 1/2 tsp	baking powder	12 mL
1/2 tsp	salt	2 mL
1 1/4 cup	milk replacement	310 mL
1/4 cup	applesauce, milk replacement or (2 eggs)	60 mL

Cream together margarine, sugar, applesauce (or eggs) and vanilla. Add dry ingredients and milk replacement alternately. Pour into greased and floured 9x13 inch (22x33 cm) pan or 2 round pans. Bake at 350°F (180°C) for 30–35 minutes. When cool cover with favourite icing.

* Coloured sprinkles can be added to the dough to create a rainbow cake.

* cocoa can be added to make a chocolate cake.

Applesauce Raisin Cake   350°

1 3/4 cup	whole wheat flour	425 mL
1/4 tsp	crème of tartar	1 mL
1/4 tsp	salt	1 mL
1 tsp	baking soda	5 mL
1 tsp	cinnamon	5 mL
1/2 tsp	cloves	2 mL
1/2 cup	raisins	125 mL
1/2 cup	milk-free margarine	125 mL
1/2 cup	honey	125 mL
1/4 cup	applesauce (1 egg)	60 mL
1 cup	sweetened applesauce	250 mL

Cream milk-free margarine and honey, add applesauce (or egg). Stir in remaining ingredients. Bake at 350°F (180°C) for approximately 35 minutes. Ice if you like or use a crumb topping.

Cakes

Brownies 375°

1 cup	milk-free margarine	250 mL
2 cups	white sugar	500 mL
2 cups	flour	500 mL
1/4 cup	cocoa	60 mL
1 tsp	vanilla	5 mL
1/4–1/2 cup	milk replacement - approximately enough to make soft cake dough (but still stiff)	60–125 mL

Cream together margarine, sugar and vanilla. Stir in flour and cocoa alternately with milk replacement. Bake at 375°F (190°C) for only 15–20 minutes. Serve with chocolate sauce and whipped topping (milk-free), frozen milk-free dessert or ice with chocolate icing.

Crumb Cake 350°

2 cups	flour	500 mL
1 cup	sugar	250 mL
1 cup	milk-free margarine	250 mL

Mix into crumbs. Take out one cup of crumbs.

To remainder add:

1/2 cup	applesauce	125 mL
2 tsp	baking powder	10 mL
1 cup	milk replacement	250 mL
1/2 tsp	cinnamon	2 mL
1 cup	raisins	250 mL

Sprinkle remaining crumbs on top and bake at 350°F (180°C) for 30 minutes.

Cakes

Matrimonial Cake (Date Cake) — 350°

1 lb	dates cooked and cooled	450 g
1 1/2 cups	flour	375 mL
1/4 tsp	salt	1 mL
1 cup	brown sugar	250 mL
1/2 tsp	baking soda	2 mL
1 tsp	baking powder	5 mL
1 1/2 to 2 cups	oatmeal	375–500 mL
1 cup	milk-free margarine melted	250 mL

Mix all ingredients except dates. Put 1/2 of mixture in bottom of 8x8 pan and press. Put cooled dates on top, cover with remaining crumbs. Bake at 350°F (180°C) for approximately 40 minutes.

Fresh Raspberry Cake — 325°

1/2 cup	milk-free margarine	125 mL
1 cup	sugar	250 mL
1/2 cup	applesauce, milk replacement (or 2 eggs)	125 mL
2 cups	flour	500 mL
2 tsp	baking powder	10 mL
2 tbsp	milk replacement	30 mL
1 cup	fresh raspberries	250 mL
1/4 tsp	salt	1 mL

Cream together margarine and sugar, add applesauce (or eggs). Add dry ingredients and milk replacement alternately. Gently fold in raspberries. Spoon batter into lightly greased 8 inch (20 cm) square pan. Bake at 325°F (160°C) for 40–50 minutes.

Fresh apricots, peaches or other berries may be used.

Cakes

Chocolate Pudding Cake 350°

Cake

1 cup	flour	250 mL
3/4 cup	white sugar	175 mL
2 tsp	baking powder	10 mL
2 tbsp	cocoa	30 mL
2–3 tbsp	milk-free margarine	30–45 mL
1/2 cup	milk replacement	125 mL
1 tsp	vanilla	5 mL
1/4 tsp	salt	1 mL

Stir together dry ingredients, work in margarine, add milk replacement and vanilla. Drop by spoonfuls into greased 8x8 inch (20x20 cm) pan.

Sauce

1 cup	brown sugar	250 mL
2–3 tbsp	cocoa	30–45 mL
1 cup	boiling water	250 mL

Stir together brown sugar and cocoa, sprinkle over batter. Pour boiling water over and bake at 350°F (180°C) for 30 minutes. Serve warm with milk-free whipped topping or milk-free frozen dessert.

Cakes

Carrot Cake 350°

3/4–1 cup	oil	175 mL–250 mL
2 cups	brown sugar	500 mL
3/4 cup	applesauce (or 3 eggs)	175 mL
1 tsp	salt	5 mL
2 cups	grated carrot	500 mL
2 cups	flour	500 mL
1 tsp	baking soda	5 mL
3 tsp	baking powder	15 mL
1 1/2 tsp	cinnamon	7 mL
1 1/2 tsp	cloves	7 mL
	raisins are optional	

Combine oil, sugar and applesauce well. (If using eggs add one at a time and beat well.) Add dry ingredients. Fold in carrots. Bake in a greased or non-stick pan at 350°F (180°C) for 45 minutes to one hour.

chapter 3

Cookies

Cookies

Chocolate Pinwheel Cookies 350°

3 cups	milk-free margarine	750 mL
2 cups	icing sugar	500 mL
2 tsp	vanilla	10 mL
6 cups	flour	1.5 L
1/2 tsp	salt	2 mL
1/2 cup	cocoa	125 mL

Blend well together margarine, icing sugar and vanilla, work in flour and salt, dough is much like shortbread. Divide dough into 2; add cocoa to one 1/2. Form dough into balls (4 white, 4 brown). Roll between sheets of waxed paper. Place one chocolate sheet on top of one white and gently roll the 2 tightly together—like a jellyroll. Chill and cut. Bake at 350°F (180°C) for 10–12 minutes.

Caramel Sandwich Cookies

graham wafers
caramel icing (cooked)

Spread icing between wafers and freeze to keep.

Cookies

Chocolate Chip/Oatmeal Cookies   375°

1 cup	milk-free margarine	250 mL
1 cup	packed brown sugar	250 mL
1 cup	white sugar	250 mL
3/4 cup	applesauce (or 2 eggs)	175 mL
2 tsp	vanilla	10 mL
1 1/3 cup	whole wheat flour*	325 mL
1 tsp	baking soda	5 mL
2 cups	rolled oats	500 mL
1 1/2 cups	chocolate chips	375 mL

*can use 1/2 whole wheat flour and 1/2 white flour

Cream margarine, sugars, and applesauce (or eggs). Stir in flour, soda and salt. Blend well. Stir in rolled oats and chocolate chips. Drop onto cookie sheets; allow some room for spreading. Bake at 375°F (190°C) for 8–10 minutes. Leave on sheet for a few minutes before removing.

Cookies

Chocolate Cake Cookies — 375°

1/3 cup	soft milk-free margarine	75 mL
1/2 cup	icing sugar	125 mL
1/4 cup	packed brown sugar	50 mL
1 tsp	vanilla	5 mL
1 cup	flour	250 mL
1/2 tsp	baking soda	2 mL
1/4 cup	cocoa	50 mL
1/2 tsp	salt	2 mL
1/4 cup	applesauce (or 1 egg)	50 mL

Beat margarine, icing sugar, and applesauce (or egg); add vanilla until light and fluffy. Add flour, baking soda, salt and cocoa. Blend well. Roll into little balls. Bake at 375°F (190°C) for 8–10 minutes.

Use chocolate chips, white sugar or icing sugar on top of cookies.

Gingerbread (old fashioned) — 350°

1 cup	vegetable shortening or milk-free margarine	250 mL
2 cups	molasses	500 mL
1/4 cup	sugar	50 mL
1 tsp	baking soda	5 mL
3 tsp	baking powder	15 mL
3 tsp	ginger	15 mL
1 1/4 tsp	salt	6 mL
7 cups	flour	1.75 L
1/2 cup	warm water or milk replacement	125 mL

Melt shortening; add molasses and warm water. Mix in dry ingredients. This dough is quite stiff and works well if done with a mixer that has a dough hook. Chill dough well. Roll out to 1/4 inch (0.5 cm) thickness on lightly floured surface, cut into shapes. Bake at 350°F (180°C) for approximately 12 minutes. Ice when cooled.

Cookies

Rolled Ginger Cookies (soft)   350°

2/3 cup	shortening or milk-free margarine	150 mL
2 cups	brown sugar	500 mL
1/2 cup	applesauce (or 2 eggs)	125 mL
1/2 cup	molasses	125 mL
3 1/2 cup	flour	875 mL
2 tsp	soda	10 mL
1 tsp	salt	5 mL
1/2 tsp	cloves	2 mL
1 tsp	cinnamon	5 mL
1 tsp	ginger	5 mL
1/2 cup	milk replacement	125 mL

Cream margarine, sugar, and applesauce (or egg) together. Add dry ingredients and milk replacement alternately to form dough. Chill dough well. Roll out on lightly floured surface and cut into rounds. Bake at 350°F (180°C) for approximately 12 minutes. Cool and ice.

Ginger Snaps   350°

1 1/4 cup	milk-free margarine	310 mL
1/2 cup	applesauce (or 2 eggs)	125 mL
3 cups	flour	750 mL
3 tsp	baking soda	15 mL
1/8 tsp	salt	0.5 mL
1 1/2 cups	sugar	375 mL
1/2 cup	molasses	125 mL
1 1/2 tsp	ginger	7 mL
1 1/2 tsp	cinnamon	7 mL
	white sugar for rolling cookies in	

Cream margarine, sugar, and applesauce (or egg). Add dry ingredients and mix well. Roll into balls and dip into sugar. Place balls on cookie sheet and bake at 350°F (180°C) 12–15 minutes. These cookies crack nicely on top.

Cookies

Gumdrop Raisin Cookies 375°

1/2 cup	milk-free margarine	125 mL
1/3 cup	brown sugar	75 mL
1/4 cup	applesauce (or 1 egg)	50 mL
2/3 cup	honey	150 mL
1 tsp	lemon flavouring (optional)	5 mL
3 cups	whole wheat flour	750 mL
1 tsp	baking soda	5 mL
1 tsp	salt	5 mL
1 cup	golden seedless raisins	250 mL
1/2 cup	very soft gumdrops cut into pieces	125 mL

Cream margarine, applesauce (or egg), honey and flavouring. Add dry ingredients a little at a time mixing well. Stir in raisins and gumdrops. Shape into roll approximately 3 inches (7.5 cm) in diameter. Chill overnight wrapped in wax paper. Slice with sharp knife. Bake at 375°F (190°C) for 8–10 minutes.

Cookies

White Cut-out Cookies 350°

1 cup	milk-free margarine	250 mL
1 cup	brown sugar	250 mL
3 cups	flour	750 mL
1/4 cup	milk replacement (or 2 eggs)	50 mL
1 tsp	vanilla - required	5 mL
1 tsp	baking soda dissolved in a little hot water	5 mL
2 tsp	crème of tartar	10 mL

Beat together the margarine, sugar, baking soda and water, vanilla and milk replacement (or egg). Add flour and crème of tartar. Do not over beat. Leave dough covered in fridge until chilled. Roll on floured surface and cut out. Bake at 350°F (180°C) for 10–12 minutes. Cool and ice.

Icing

icing sugar
vanilla (optional)

Add water and beat to a smooth spreadable consistency. This icing will harden on cookies as it cools. Freeze cookies with wax paper between.

Cookies

Candy Cookies   350°

* when using cut up jelly candy, mix in flour so they don't stick together.

1 cup	milk-free margarine	250 mL
1 cup	brown sugar	250 mL
1 tsp	vanilla	5 mL
1/4 cup	applesauce (or 1 egg)	50 mL
1 1/4 cup	flour	310 mL
1/2 tsp	baking soda	2 mL
1 cup	rolled oats	250 mL
1/2 tsp	baking powder	2 mL
1/4 tsp	salt	1 mL
1 cup	chopped soft jelly candies (chocolate chips or raisins)	250 mL

Cream first 4 ingredients. Add remaining dry ingredients, stir in candy. Drop by teaspoon onto greased cookie sheet. Bake at 350°F (180°C) for 12–15 minutes.

Note - black jelly candies are often too strong to be used.

Cookies

Healthy Snack Cookies 350°

1 cup	milk-free margarine	250 mL
3/4 cup	brown sugar	175 mL
1/2 cup	applesauce (or 2 eggs)	125 mL
1 tsp	vanilla	5 mL
1 cup	coconut (optional) - can use oatmeal	250 mL
1 cup	raisins	250 mL
1/2 cup	sunflower seeds*	125 mL
1/2 cup	flax seeds*	125 mL
1/4 cup	sesame seeds*	50 mL
1/2 cup	chocolate chips	125 mL
2 cups	whole wheat flour	500 mL
1 tsp	baking powder	5 mL
1 tsp	salt	5 mL
1 tsp	baking soda	5 mL

Cream margarine and sugar, add applesauce (or eggs), beat until smooth. Add remaining dry ingredients. Drop by teaspoon onto cookie sheets. Bake at 350°F (180°C) for 12 minutes.

* Sunflower and sesame can be very difficult to find that do not have nut warnings. Omit if this happens. Increase oatmeal if you like, or a safe cereal.

Cookies

Oatmeal Cookies 375°

2 cups	milk-free margarine	500 mL
2 cups	white sugar	500 mL
2 cups	brown sugar	500 mL
1/2 to 3/4 cup	applesauce (or 2 eggs)	125–175 mL
2 tsp	vanilla	10 mL
4 cups	flour*	1 L
3 cups	oatmeal	750 mL
1 tsp	salt	5 mL
2 tsp	baking powder	10 mL
2 tsp	baking soda	10 mL
	chocolate chips (optional)	

*can use 1/2 whole wheat flour and 1/2 white flour

Cream together margarine, applesauce (or eggs), sugar and vanilla. Add flour, baking powder, baking soda and salt. Stir in oatmeal and chocolate chips—if using. Drop by spoonfuls on cookie sheet. For chewy cookies bake at 375°F (190°C) for only 8 minutes. Cookies will barely be brown but will remain chewy. Cool on pan for a couple of minutes before removing.

Cookies

Old Fashioned Sugar Cookies — 375°

1 cup	milk-free margarine	250 mL
1/2 cup	brown sugar	125 mL
1/2 cup	white sugar	125 mL
1/4 cup	applesauce (or 1 egg)	50 mL
1 tsp	vanilla	5 mL
2 cups	flour	500 mL
1 tsp	baking soda	5 mL
1 tsp	crème of tartar	5 mL
	icing sugar	
	jam	

Cream margarine, sugars, applesauce (or egg) and vanilla. Stir in dry ingredients. Chill dough. Roll dough to 1/4 inch (0.5 cm) thickness, cut out with round cookie cutter. You can take a smaller cookie cutter and cut out the centers. Place on cookie sheets. Bake at 375°F (190°C) for 10–12 minutes. Icing sugar can be sifted over top. Jam can be spread between cookies if you like.

Whipped Shortbread — 350°

1 cup	milk-free margarine	250 mL
1 1/2 cups	pastry flour (or regular)	375 mL
1/2 cup	icing sugar	125 mL

Combine all ingredients, beat for 10 minutes, do not under beat. Roll into balls or drop by small teaspoon and put on cookie sheet. Decorate with maraschino cherry or use food colouring if you like. Bake at 350°F (180°C) for 10–12 minutes.

Cookies

No-Bake Chocolate Cookies

1 cup	sugar	250 mL
1/4 cup	milk replacement	50 mL
1/4 cup	milk-free margarine	50 mL
3 tbsp	cocoa	45 mL
1/2 cup	syrup	125 mL
1 1/2 cups	oatmeal	375 mL
1/2 cup	coconut (optional)	125 mL
1/2 tsp	vanilla	2 mL

Mix first five ingredients, bring to a boil, and add vanilla. Pour over oatmeal and coconut. Place spoonfuls on waxpaper until cool. Can be pressed into a greased pan as well.

Cinnamon Twists — 350°

2 cups	milk-free margarine	500 mL
1/2 cup	applesauce or milk replacement (2 eggs)	125 mL
5 cups	flour	1.25 L
2 tsp	baking powder	10 mL
1 cup	milk replacement	250 mL

Sugar coating

1 cup	white sugar	250 mL
3 tbsp	cinnamon (optional)	45 mL

Cut margarine, flour and baking powder together like for piecrust, add applesauce (or eggs) and milk replacement, mix together well. Chill dough.

Roll out portions but instead of using flour use sugar mixture with or without cinnamon. Cut dough into triangles or square roll up; roll in sugar to coat well. Bake at 350°F (180°C) for 15 minutes.

If using only sugar the dough can be coloured with food or icing colour.

Cookies

Apple Oatmeal Cookies — 375°

1/2 cup	milk-free margarine	125 mL
1 1/2 cups	oatmeal	375 mL
3/4 cup	white flour	175 mL
3/4 cup	whole wheat flour	175 mL
1/2 cup	brown sugar	125 mL
1 tsp	baking powder	5 mL
1/4 tsp	baking soda	1 mL
1/2 tsp	salt	2 mL
1 1/2 tsp	cinnamon	7 mL
1/2 cup	washed raisins	125 mL
1 cup	grated apple	250 mL
1/2 cup	honey or syrup	125 mL
1/3 cup	milk replacement (2 eggs) or applesauce	75 mL

Cream margarine with sugar, honey and milk replacement (or eggs). Stir in apples and raisins. Stir in dry ingredients. Drop by spoonfuls on baking sheet. Bake at 375°F (190°C) for 10 minutes.

Cookie Monsters — 350°

1/4 cup	milk-free margarine	50 mL
1 cup	brown sugar	250 mL
1/2 cup	flour	125 mL
1/2 tsp	baking powder	2 mL
1 tsp	cinnamon	5 mL
1/2 tsp	salt	2 mL
3 tbsp	water	45 mL
1 1/2 cups	oatmeal	375 mL
1/2–3/4 cup	raisins	125–175 mL

Cream together the margarine, brown sugar, and water. Stir together remaining dry. Mix in raisins. Drop by spoonfuls onto cookie sheet. Bake at 350°F (180°C) for 10–12 minutes.

Cookies

Oatmeal Date Cookies   350°

1 cup	milk-free margarine	250 mL
1 cup	brown sugar	250 mL
1/2 cup	milk replacement	125 mL
2 cups	oatmeal	500 mL
2 cups	flour*	500 mL
1 tsp	baking soda	5 mL

*can use 1/2 whole wheat flour and 1/2 white flour

Filling

2 cups	dates	500 mL
1/2 cup	sugar	125 mL
1 tbsp	milk-free margarine	15 mL
3/4 cup	cold water	175 mL
1 tsp	lemon juice	5 mL

Cream margarine, sugar and milk replacement and add dry ingredients. Roll out dough and cut into circles with or without centers. Bake at 350°F (180°C) for 10–12 minutes. Cook date mixture until soft—cool. When both cookies and dates have cooled spread cookies with filling and place another cookie on top.

Cookies

Peanut Butter FREE Cookies 375°

1 cup	brown sugar	250 mL
1/2 cup	peanut butter replacement - 100% peanut/nut free	125 mL
1/2 cup	milk-free margarine	125 mL
1/4 cup	applesauce (1 egg or milk replacement)	50 mL
1 1/4 cup	flour	310 mL
3/4 tsp	baking soda	3 mL
1/2 tsp	baking powder	2 mL

Mix sugar, peanut butter replacement - 100% peanut/nut free, margarine and applesauce. Stir in remaining ingredients. Cover and refrigerate for 2–3 hours. Shape dough into balls and place on ungreased cookie sheet. Flatten with a fork dipped in flour. Bake at 375°F (190°C) for 10 minutes.

Alternative - shape dough into balls and push thumb into ball to make an indentation. Fill with your favourite jam or jelly.

Peanut butter replacements can be found in grocery stores usually in the section which carries peanut butter and jam. These products are nut free and produced in nut free facilities. The products taste very close to peanut butter.

Cookies

Double Chocolate Chip Cookies 350°

1 1/4 cups	milk-free margarine	310 mL
2 cups	sugar	500 mL
1/2 cup	milk replacement/applesauce (or 2 eggs)	125 mL
2 tsp	vanilla	10 mL
2 cups	flour	500 mL
3/4 cup	cocoa	175 mL
1 tsp	soda	5 mL
2 cups	chocolate chips	500 mL

Cream margarine and sugar, add milk replacement (or eggs). Mix together the dry ingredients. Stir together with the creamed mixture and add chocolate chips. Drop by spoonfuls onto cookie sheet. Bake at 350°F (180°C) for approx 8–10 minutes. Take cookies out when they have puffed up, do not over bake.

chapter **4**

Desserts, Pies & Crisps

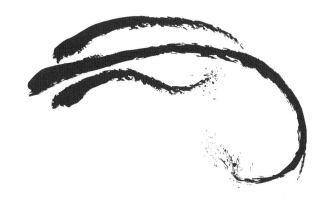

Desserts, Pies and Crisps

Apple Crisp with Marshmallows 350°

3 cups	sliced, peeled apples	750 mL
1/4 cup	washed raisins	50 mL
1/4 cup	water	50 mL
3/4 cup	flour	175 mL
1/2 cup	sugar	125 mL
1/2 tsp	cinnamon	2 mL
1/4 tsp	salt	1 mL
1/2 cup	milk-free margarine	125 mL
1 1/2 cups	miniature white marshmallows	375 mL

Place apples, raisins, and water in a 9x13 inch (22x33 cm) baking dish. Mix flour, sugar, cinnamon and salt. Cut in margarine to form crumbs. Sprinkle over apples. Bake at 350°F (180°C) for 30 minutes or until apples are tender. Sprinkle on marshmallows. Broil until brown. Serve hot.

Desserts, Pies and Crisps

Pumpkin Dessert   325°

1	pkg miniature white marshmallows	1
3 cups	fresh pumpkin or 3 1/2 cups (875 mL) canned	750 mL
1/2 cup	brown sugar	125 mL
2 tsp	cinnamon	10 mL
1 tsp	ginger	5 mL
1 tsp	cloves	5 mL
dash	pepper (optional)	dash
2 cups	whipped topping - milk-free	500 mL

Base

4 cups	graham wafer crumbs	1 L
1/2 cup	milk-free margarine	125 mL
1/2 cup	sugar	125 mL
1/2 tsp	salt	2 mL

Press all but one cup of base mixture into well-greased 9x13 inch (22x23 cm) pan. Bake base at 325°F (160°C) for 10 minutes. Cool.

Melt marshmallows in double boiler, stir often. Remove from heat and add pumpkin, sugar, and spices. Mix well and cool for 1 hour. Fold in milk-free whipped topping. Pour mixture over crumb base and sprinkle with saved crumbs. Chill and serve.

Do not leave this dessert out of fridge for a long time.

You may have to vary recipe a little depending on whether you use frozen non-dairy whipped topping or one that you prepare yourself.

Desserts, Pies and Crisps

Strawberry Dessert 350°

1	box or pkg non-dairy dessert whip	1
12 oz	strawberries	340 mL
2 cups	graham crumbs	500 mL
1/2 cup	milk-free margarine	125 mL
1/4 tsp	salt	1 mL
1 large pkg	strawberry jelly dessert powder	1
1 1/2 cups	miniature marshmallows	375 mL

Make jelly dessert according to directions and add strawberries—cool. Combine crumbs, salt and margarine and spread into lightly greased pan. Bake at 350°F (180°C) for 5–10 minutes—cool. Prepare whip; add 2/3 of jelly dessert mixture, blend well. Pour into cooled crust. Put into fridge and let set. When stiff, pour remaining jelly dessert over dessert. Keep chilled, serve chilled.

* Any fruit or jelly dessert powder can be used.

Shortbread Tart Shells 275°

1 cup	milk-free margarine	250 mL
1/2 cup	icing sugar	125 mL
1 3/4 cups	flour	425 mL

Blend together, divide into small balls. Press into tart tins and bake at 275°F (140°C) for 20–25 minutes. Store and use when needed. These are fragile so store with care to get maximum use out of all of them. Can be frozen.

Desserts, Pies and Crisps

Variation of Tart Shells 350°

1/2 cup	cornstarch	125 mL
1/2 cup	icing sugar	125 mL
1 cup	flour	250 mL
3/4 cup	milk-free margarine	175 mL

Sift cornstarch, sugar and flour together. Blend in margarine, mixing until soft (can be whipped). Form in small muffin tins or tart tins. Bake at 350°F (180°C) for 10–15 minutes. Can be frozen.

Fudge Sundae Pie

1/4 cup	corn syrup	50 mL
2 tbsp	brown sugar	30 mL
3 tbsp	milk-free margarine	45 mL
2 1/2 cups	rice crispie cereal	625 mL
1/4 cup	fudge sauce	50 mL
3 tbsp	corn syrup	45 mL
1	container milk-free frozen vanilla dessert	1

Cook 1/4 cup corn syrup, brown sugar and margarine in medium saucepan; cook over low heat, stirring occasionally until mixture begins to boil. Remove from heat. Add rice crispies, stir until well coated. Press evenly in 9 inch (22 cm) pie pan to form crust. Mix together fudge sauce and 3 tbsp corn syrup. Spread 1/2 over crust. Freeze until firm. Allow vanilla frozen dessert to soften slightly. Spoon into frozen piecrust, spread evenly. Freeze until firm. Let stand for 10 minutes prior to serving. Warm remaining chocolate fudge sauce and pour over top.

Desserts, Pies and Crisps

Pie Dough with Shortening

1 lb	shortening	450 g
6 cups	flour	1.5 L
2 tsp	salt	10 mL
1 cup	cold water	250 mL
pinch	baking powder	pinch

Cut shortening into flour, salt and baking powder. Add water to make soft dough. Roll out with a small amount of flour. Fill with favourite fruit filling.

Caramel Dumplings   350°

Sauce

1 cup	brown sugar	250 mL
1 1/2 cups	water	375 mL
2 tbsp	milk-free margarine	30 mL

Caramelize brown sugar and margarine. Add water and boil for 2 minutes.

Batter

1/2 cup	white sugar	125 mL
2 tbsp	milk-free margarine	30 mL
1/2 cup	milk replacement	125 mL
1 cup	flour	250 mL
1 tsp	baking powder	5 mL
1/8 tsp	salt	0.5 mL

Cream sugar and margarine and add milk replacement. Stir in flour, baking powder and salt. Drop by spoonfuls into caramel syrup and bake at 350°F (180°C) for 30 minutes.

Desserts, Pies and Crisps

Chocolate Cherry Crunchie — 350°

Crust & topping

1 cup	flour	250 mL
3/4 cup	brown sugar	175 mL
3/4 cup	rolled oats	175 mL
1/4 cup	cocoa	50 mL
1/4 tsp	salt	1 mL
1/2 cup	milk-free margarine	125 mL

Fruit mixture

1	21 oz can cherry pie filling brandy (optional)	1

Combine flour, brown sugar, rolled oats, cocoa and salt. Using pastry blender or fork cut in margarine until nice and crumbly. Press 1 cup of mixture into bottom of ungreased 9 inch (22 cm) square pan. Spoon pie filling over crust. Sprinkle remaining crumb mixture evenly over cherries, press lightly into filling. Bake at 350°F (180°C) for 25–30 minutes. Serve warm.

Desserts, Pies and Crisps

Blueberry Tea Ring   350°

Tea Ring

1 1/2 cups	flour	375 mL
2 tsp	baking powder	10 mL
1/4 tsp	salt	1 mL
3/4 cup	sugar	175 mL
1/4 cup	milk-free margarine - softened	50 mL
1/4 cup	applesauce (or 1 egg)	50 mL
1/2 cup	milk replacement	125 mL
3 cups	frozen blueberries - do not thaw	750 mL

Topping

1/3 cup	flour	75 mL
1/2 cup	brown sugar	125 mL
1/2 tsp	cinnamon	2 mL
1/4 cup	milk-free margarine	50 mL

Cream 1/4 cup margarine, sugar, add applesauce (or egg). Alternately add dry ingredients and milk replacement, mix well. Pour 2/3 of batter into greased ring pan. Spread with frozen blueberries. Carefully spread remaining batter. Sprinkle crumble mixture over top and bake at 350°F (180°C) for 30–35 minutes.

Desserts, Pies and Crisps

Raisin Pie Filling   350°

1 cup	water	250 mL
2 cups	washed raisins	500 mL
1 cup	white sugar	250 mL
1 tbsp	lemon juice	15 mL
2 tbsp	milk-free margarine	30 mL
3 tbsp	cornstarch	45 mL
1/4 cup	cold water	50 mL
1 tsp	vanilla	5 mL
	pastry for double pie crust	

Boil first 5 ingredients for 10–15 minutes. Mix cornstarch with cold water and add to raisin mixture, cook until thick. Take off heat and add vanilla. Pour into prepared shell and bake at 350°F (180°C) for 15–20 minutes. This can also be used for raisin tarts.

Sweet Apple Turnover   425°

1	refrigerator pie crust - milk, egg free (or home made)	1
2–3	tart apples, peeled and finely chopped (or other fruit)	2–3
1/3 cup	packed brown sugar	75 mL
1/2 tsp	ground cinnamon (optional)	2 mL
4 tsp	milk-free margarine	20 mL
2 tbsp	milk replacement	30 mL
2 tbsp	sugar	30 mL

Combine apple, cinnamon, brown sugar, and toss to mix. Roll pie crust and cut into 16 squares. Place 1 tbsp of fruit mixture into each square, dot with margarine. Fold to cover and form triangle. Brush edges with milk replacement to seal. Sprinkle with sugar. Bake at 425°F (220°C) for 10 minutes. Drizzle with icing if you choose.

Desserts, Pies and Crisps

Blueberry/Fruit Crumb Cake   350°

Crumbs

1/4 cup	flour	50 mL
1/4 cup	sugar	50 mL
1/2 tsp	cinnamon (optional)	2 mL
6 tbsp	milk-free margarine	90 mL

Cake

1/4 cup	milk-free margarine	50 mL
1/2 cup	sugar	125 mL
1/4 cup	applesauce (1 egg, or milk replacement)	50 mL
1 cup	flour	250 mL
1/2 tsp	baking powder	2 mL
1/4 tsp	salt	1 mL
1/3 cup	milk replacement	75 mL

Topping

2 cups	blueberries or fruit of choice	500 mL

Combine first 3 ingredients together to make crumbs. Cream margarine, sugar, and applesauce (or egg). Add flour and liquids alternately. Put into pan and smooth flat. Layer with blueberries. Sprinkle crumbs on top. Bake at 350°F (180°C) for 40–45 minutes.

Crumb topping can be doubled if you like the topping to be thicker.

Desserts, Pies and Crisps

Rhubarb Bavarian Dessert 350°

1 cup	flour	250 mL
1/4 tsp	salt	1 mL
2 tbsp	sugar	30 mL
1/2 cup	softened milk-free margarine	125 mL
4 cups	well washed chopped red rhubarb (or fruit of choice)	1 L
1/4 cup	water (less if fruit is not rhubarb and has a higher amount of liquid naturally)	50 mL
1 1/4 cup	sugar	300 mL
2	envelopes unflavoured gelatine (mixed with red food colouring if you like and 1/2 cup cold water)	2
1 1/4 cup	milk-free whipped topping	300 mL

Combine flour, salt and sugar. Cut margarine into dry mixture until it resembles coarse crumbs. Spread mixture evenly into 9x13 (22x33 cm) pan. Bake at 350°F (180°C) for 10–12 minutes or until lightly brown—set to cool. Combine rhubarb, 1/4 cup water and sugar in large saucepan. Simmer until fruit is tender, stirring occasionally. Add gelatine mixture to hot rhubarb and stir until dissolved. Chill until partially set. Fold in whipped topping. Put into chilled base and chill again until firm (3–4 hours).

Desserts, Pies and Crisps

Rhubarb Crunch   350°

1 cup	flour	250 mL
3/4 cup	rolled oats	175 mL
1 cup	brown sugar	250 mL
1/2 cup	melted milk-free margarine	125 mL
1 tsp	cinnamon (optional)	5 mL
4 cups	well washed, chopped into small pieces red rhubarb (other fruit can be substituted)	1 L
1 cup	sugar	250 mL
2 tbsp	corn starch	30 mL
1 cup	water	250 mL
1 tsp	vanilla	5 mL

Combine first 5 ingredients to make crumbs. Press 1/2 into a greased 9x13 (22x33 cm) Pyrex dish and cover with rhubarb. Cook sugar, cornstarch, water and vanilla until mixture is thick and clear. Pour this over the rhubarb. Top with remaining crumbs. Bake at 350°F (180°C) for approximately 1 hour.

Desserts, Pies and Crisps

Christmas Pudding

1 cup	grated carrots	250 mL
1 cup	grated potatoes	250 mL
1 1/2 cups	suet	375 mL
1 1/2 cups	brown sugar	375 mL
2 cups	seedless raisins	500 mL
1 cup	currants	250 mL
1 1/2 cups	cherries	375 mL
1 cup	mixed fruit	250 mL
1/2	lemon (optional)	1/2
1	orange (optional)	1
3/4 cup	flour	175 mL
2–3 tsp	cinnamon	10–15 mL
1–2 tsp	cloves	5–10 mL
1 tsp	salt	5 mL
1 tsp	soda	5 mL

Mix carrots, potato, brown sugar and fruit. If using the lemon and orange put through a food processor to chop finely. Sift flour, spices, salt and soda together. Add to previous mixture. Place in sterilized canning jars 3/4 full. Steam for 3 hours, remove from canner and store until needed. *Check to make sure all jars have sealed properly, refrigerate any open jars or left overs. This pudding heats nicely in a slow cooker. Heat on medium-high for 3–4 hours.

* If doubling the recipe only increase the flour by 1/4 cup. This recipe is very adaptable to suit different tastes.

Desserts, Pies and Crisps

Rum Sauce for Christmas Pudding

1 cup	brown sugar	250 mL
1 tbsp	grated lemon rind	15 mL
1 1/2 cups	boiling water	375 mL
1 tbsp	milk-free margarine	15 mL
1 tbsp	cornstarch	15 mL
3 tbsp	lemon juice	45 mL
1/4–1/2 cup	dark rum or flavouring to your taste	60–125 mL
	sprinkle of salt	

Combine sugar and lemon rind with water; add margarine and heat to a boil. Mix cornstarch with lemon juice and add to mixture. Cook for 8 minutes, remove from heat, strain if necessary, and add rum and salt. Serve hot with pudding.

White Hard Sauce for Christmas Pudding

1/3 cup	milk-free margarine	75 mL
1 cup	icing sugar	250 mL
3/4–1 tsp	vanilla	3–5 mL
1 tbsp	milk replacement	15 mL

Cream margarine, beat in sugar gradually and continue beating until fluffy. Add flavouring and milk replacement. Chill. Serve with Christmas pudding and hot rum sauce.

Desserts, Pies and Crisps

Frozen Dessert Squares

20	chocolate cookies with vanilla filling (milk, egg, nut free - they do exist)	20
1	container softened vanilla frozen dessert	1
1	pkg butterscotch instant pudding mix (optional)	1
2 cups	milk-free whipped topping	500 mL
	chocolate syrup or sauce	

Crush cookies and cover bottom of pan. Mix whipped topping, pudding mix and softened frozen dessert. Pour over cookies and freeze in pan. Sprinkle with more crushed cookies if you like. Drizzle with chocolate sauce, cover with foil and freeze.

Unbaked Coconut Slice

	whole graham wafers	
1/2 cup	milk-free margarine	125 mL
1 cup	brown sugar	250 mL
1/3 cup	milk replacement	75 mL
1 cup	finely chopped sweetened coconut	250 mL
1 cup	crushed graham wafer crumbs	250 mL

Icing for Unbaked Coconut Slice

1/2 cup	milk-free margarine	125 mL
1 1/4 cup	icing sugar	300 mL
1 tsp	vanilla	5 mL
1/8–1/4 cup	milk replacement	25–50 mL

Line 8 inch (20 cm) pan with whole graham wafers. Melt margarine and add brown sugar and milk replacement. Bring just to a boil and remove from heat. Add coconut and crushed graham wafers. Spread mixture over whole wafers and press in. Cover with whole graham wafers. Cool. Beat margarine, icing sugar, vanilla and milk replacement until creamy. Spread over slice and cool.

Desserts, Pies and Crisps

Berry Crisp 350°

4 cups	fresh berries	1 L
2 tsp	lemon juice	10 mL
1/3 cup	sugar	75 mL

Topping

1 cup	rolled oats	250 mL
2/3 cup	brown sugar	150 mL
2/3 cup	flour	150 mL
1/2 cup	milk-free margarine	125 mL

Grease baking dish, arrange berries, sprinkle with sugar and lemon juice. Cut margarine into dry ingredients to make a crumble. Put on top of berries. Bake at 350°F (180°C) for 25 minutes or until golden.

* If you double the topping it can be used as a bottom and the other 1/2 as topping.

Desserts, Pies and Crisps

Fruit Square — 350°

2 cups	flour	500 mL
2 tbsp	sugar	30 mL
1 tsp	baking powder	5 mL
1/4 tsp	salt	1 mL
1 cup	milk-free margarine	250 mL
1/4 cup	applesauce (1 egg)	50 mL
1/2 cup	milk replacement	125 mL
1 tsp	vanilla	5 mL
2	tins of apple pie filling or home-made - approximately 2–3 cups	2
2 tsp	cinnamon	10 mL

Blend flour, sugar, baking powder and salt. Cut in margarine as for pastry. In bowl beat applesauce (or egg) and vanilla, add to dry mixture. Roll out 1/2 to fit cookie sheet, spread with filling, sprinkle cinnamon on top. Roll out other 1/2 of dough and place over filling. Cut air vents. Bake at 350°F (180°C) for 25–30 minutes.

Desserts, Pies and Crisps

Mocha Fudge Brownies with Icing — 300°

Cake

1/2 cup	milk-free margarine	125 mL
1 cup	white sugar	250 mL
1/2 cup	applesauce (2 eggs or milk replacement)	125 mL
3	squares of unsweetened chocolate or use cocoa	3
	pinch of salt	
2/3 cup	flour	150 mL
1 tsp	vanilla	5 mL

Cream margarine and sugar, add applesauce (or eggs). Melt chocolate squares, add to creamed mixture, and mix well. Add vanilla. Stir in flour and salt. Pour into greased and lightly floured 8x8 inch (20x20 cm) pan. Bake at 300°F (150°C) for 35 minutes or until done. Remove from oven but do not remove from pan!

Icing

1 tbsp	milk-free margarine	15 mL
1 tbsp	cocoa	15 mL
1 cup	icing sugar	250 mL
	brewed coffee - cool	

Cream margarine; add cocoa and icing sugar, mix well. Add enough coffee to make a thin paste. Cover cake thoroughly to edge of pan, allowing icing to run down sides.

The mocha fudge taste occurs when the thin icing meets the warm cake.

Desserts, Pies and Crisps

Trifle

2–3 cups	custard powder or cooked pudding	500–750 mL
1	pkg jelly dessert powder - you choose or co-ordinate with fruit	1
1	canned fruit of choice - drained	1
1	whipped topping	1
1	white cake - home-made or from cake mix (some are safe, leave out eggs and use milk replacement)	1

Make jelly dessert according to box. Break up cake into jelly dessert powder and let set. When jelly base is set place drained fruit on top. Make custard according to package using milk replacement. Pour on top of fruit and refrigerate. Just before serving top with whipped topping.

Topping for any Fruit Crisp

2 cups	oatmeal	500 mL
1 cup	flour - can use whole wheat	250 mL
1 cup	milk-free margarine	250 mL
2 cups	brown sugar	500 mL

Cut margarine into dry ingredients until crumbly. Use for bottom and top of crisp.

Desserts, Pies and Crisps

Tapioca Pudding

3 1/2 cups	milk replacement	875 mL
2 tbsp	brown sugar	30 mL
2 tbsp	white sugar	30 mL
1/2 cup	pearl tapioca	125 mL

Stir together all ingredients in a double boiler. Bring the pudding to a boil over medium heat, stirring constantly. Reduce heat and cook for approximately 35 to 40 minutes, stirring often.

* Most cooked puddings can be made with milk replacement. You can add extra vanilla to enhance the flavour or add fruit such as bananas. This can be served as a pudding or used as a cream pie. Milk-free whipped topping can be used on top.

chapter 5

Icing & Frostings

Icing and Frostings

Cooked Icing

5 tbsp	flour	75 mL
1 cup	milk replacement	250 mL
1 cup	white sugar	250 mL
1 cup	milk-free margarine	250 mL
2 tsp	vanilla - increase if you like	10 mL

Slowly stir together flour and milk replacement being careful to avoid lumps forming. Cook flour and milk replacement, stirring until it forms a ball. Remove from stove and cool. Cream margarine, sugar and vanilla, beat until smooth. Add to first mixture, beat until it resembles whipped topping. This makes a large amount of icing and can be stored for up to 2 weeks in a sealed container.

White Icing

2/3 cup	milk-free margarine	150 mL
4 cups	icing sugar	1 L
1 tsp	vanilla	5 mL
2–4 tbsp	milk replacement	30–60 mL

Cream margarine, gradually add icing sugar, beating well. Beat in vanilla and milk replacement—enough to make desirable spreading.

Icing variations:

Substitute 1–2 tsp (5–10 mL) lemon, orange or flavouring of choice for vanilla.

Coffee cream icing: 1 1/2 tsp (7 mL) instant coffee instead of 2 tbsp (30 mL) milk replacement.

Icing and Frostings

Bakery Shop Icing

1/2 cup	softened milk-free margarine	125 mL
1/4 cup	solid vegetable shortening	60 mL
3 cups	icing sugar	750 mL
2 tbsp	corn syrup (optional)	30 mL
2 tsp	milk replacement	10 mL
	vanilla (optional)	

Beat margarine and shortening until creamy. Gradually add icing sugar, continue beating. Add syrup and milk replacement, beat until smooth.

Caramel Icing

1/4 cup	milk-free margarine	60 mL
1 cup	brown sugar	250 mL
2 tbsp	milk replacement	30 mL
	icing sugar	

Melt margarine, add sugar and milk replacement. Bring to a boil, remove from heat and cool for 5 minutes. Add 1 tsp vanilla. Beat in enough icing sugar to make a nice smooth spreading icing.

Note - this icing hardens quickly and works best when it is warm.

Icing and Frostings

Boiled Icing

3 tbsp	milk-free margarine	45 mL
1 cup	brown sugar	250 mL
1/4 tsp	salt	1 mL
1/3 cup	milk replacement	75 mL
1 tsp	vanilla	5 mL
	icing sugar	

Combine sugar, milk replacement and salt in double boiler. Bring to boil. Cook slowly until slightly thickened. Remove from heat. Add margarine and vanilla. Cool slightly. Add enough icing sugar to make icing, beat until smooth. Using icing as soon as possible as it will harden and not spread.

Icing for Cut-out Cookies

icing sugar
vanilla (optional)

Add water and beat to a smooth spreadable consistency. This icing will harden on cookies as it cools. Freeze cookies with wax paper between.

Icing and Frostings

Mocha Fudge Brownie Icing

1 tbsp	milk-free margarine	15 mL
1 tbsp	cocoa	15 mL
1 cup	icing sugar	250 mL
	brewed coffee - cool	

Cream margarine; add cocoa and icing sugar, mix well. Add enough coffee to make a thin paste. Cover cake thoroughly to edge of pan, allowing icing to run down sides.

The mocha fudge taste occurs when the thin icing meets the warm cake.

Coffee Whipped Topping Frosting

3 cups	milk-free frozen whipped topping	750 mL
	thawed or milk-free whipped topping	
1 tbsp	instant coffee granules	15 mL

Sprinkle instant coffee granules over whipped topping, gently fold into topping only until granules disappear and topping has a speckled look. This is tasty on brownies or chocolate cake.

Cooked pudding mix can be added to whipped topping prior to whipping to make a nice icing or for an addition to hot cocoa.

Icing and Frostings

Chocolate Icing

1 cup	sugar	250 mL
1/3 cup	milk-free margarine	75 mL
1/3 cup	milk replacement	75 mL
1 cup	chocolate chips or cocoa to taste	250 mL
1 tsp	vanilla	5 mL

Melt margarine over medium heat, add sugar, milk replacement, and vanilla and bring to a boil for 1 minute. Remove from heat and stir in chocolate chips.

The Best Icing

1/2 cup	milk-free margarine	125 mL
3 cups	icing sugar	750 mL
2 tsp	vanilla	10 mL
2 tbsp	milk replacement	30 mL

Beat together margarine and 2 cups (500 mL) of icing sugar, beat until nice and smooth, add vanilla. Slowly add remaining icing sugar alternately with the milk replacement.

*add 1/3 cup (75 mL) sifted cocoa for chocolate icing and increase milk replacement to make the desired consistency.

Icing and Frostings

Fudge Icing

3 tbsp	melted milk-free margarine	45 mL
1/4 cup	cocoa	60 mL
1/4 cup	milk replacement	60 mL
1/2 tsp	vanilla	2 mL
2–3 cups	icing sugar	500–750 mL

Beat together margarine and cocoa. Alternately add icing sugar and milk replacement. Add vanilla.

Marshmallow Frosting

1	package marshmallows	1
3/4 cup	milk replacement	175 mL
1	large package milk-free whipped topping	1

Melt together the marshmallows and the milk replacement in double boiler, set aside stirring to keep smooth. Whip topping according to directions, fold into melted marshmallows. Use for between layers or for frosting.

When using milk-free whipped topping for frostings do not over beat as it can become too stiff to spread.

Icing and Frostings

Berry Glaze for Cake

1 box	strawberry or raspberry jelly dessert powder	1
1 cup	boiling water	250 mL
1	package frozen strawberries or raspberries	1

Dissolve jelly dessert powder in boiling water. Add frozen berries and stir gently until the berries separate. Cool and spoon over cooled cake. Cool to set glaze.

any flavour of jelly dessert powder and the same fruit can be used.

chapter 6

Candy & Special Sweet Treats

Candy/Special Sweet Treats

Caramel Corn

6 quarts	popped corn (seeds removed)	5.5 L
2 2/3 cups	brown sugar	650 mL
1 1/2 cups	milk-free margarine	375 mL
1 cup	cane syrup	250 mL
1 tsp	vanilla (optional)	5 mL

Boil sugar, margarine and syrup to hard ball stage, add vanilla. Pour over popcorn. Mix well and spread on cookie sheet covered with wax paper. Let set and break apart. This treat freezes well.

Popcorn Balls

2 cups	cane syrup	500 mL
1 cup	white sugar	250 mL
1 tbsp	vinegar	15 mL
1 tbsp	milk-free margarine	15 mL
1/8 tsp	salt (optional)	0.5 mL
1/4 tsp	baking soda	1 mL
20 cups	popped corn (seeds removed) - salted optional	5 L

Boil syrup, sugar, vinegar and margarine until it reaches soft ball stage—about 10 minutes. Add baking soda—<u>caution: mixture will foam</u>. Pour over popped corn and form into balls as soon as mixture is cool enough to handle. Use margarine on hands or dip hands into cold water to form balls if too sticky. These freeze well.

Candy/Special Sweet Treats

Marshmallow Popcorn Balls

1	regular pkg marshmallows	1
1/2–3/4 cup	milk-free margarine	125–175 mL
1 pkg	safe gumdrops	1
4 quarts	popped corn (seeds removed)	3.5 L

Melt marshmallows and margarine in double boiler or in microwave. Stir until smooth. Pour over popcorn and gumdrops. Form into balls, let set on wax paper. These freeze well.

Coloured Popcorn Balls

2 cups	corn syrup	500 mL
1 cup	white sugar	250 mL
1 tbsp	vinegar	15 mL
1/4 tsp	baking soda	1 mL
1 tbsp	milk-free margarine	15 mL
1/8 tsp	salt (optional)	0.5 mL
1	small pkg jelly dessert powder - flavour of choice	1
20 cups	popped corn (seeds removed) - salted optional	5 L

Boil syrup, sugar, vinegar and margarine until it reaches the soft ball stage, approximately 10 minutes. Add jelly dessert powder and then baking soda—<u>caution: mixture will foam</u>. Pour hot syrup over popped corn and form into balls when mixture is cool enough to handle. Use margarine on hands or dip hands into cold water to form balls if too sticky. These freeze well.

Candy/Special Sweet Treats

Graham Wafer Crumbs 350°

4 3/4 cups	white or whole wheat flour	1.25 L
1/4 cup	honey	60 mL
1/4 cup	brown sugar	60 mL
1 tsp	salt	5 mL
2 tsp	baking powder	10 mL
1 cup	milk-free margarine	250 mL
3/4 cup	milk replacement	175 mL
1 tsp	vanilla	5 mL
1 tsp	baking soda	5 mL

Mix together and spread on cookie sheets. Bake at 350°F (180°C) for approximately 10–15 minutes. Crumb in blender when cool or break up and eat as a cracker.

Fudge

1/2 cup	milk replacement	125 mL
1/3 cup	cocoa	75 mL
2 cups	sugar	500 mL
1/2 cup	milk-free margarine	125 mL
1 cup	flour	250 mL
1/2 tsp	vanilla (optional)	2 mL

Stir together all ingredients except flour and vanilla. Boil until the mixture reaches the soft ball stage. Remove from heat; add a little vanilla if you choose and flour. Stir until smooth and thick. Pour into greased pan, cool and cut.

* Add raisins, coconut or marshmallows.

Candy/Special Sweet Treats

Maple Cream Fudge

4 cups	brown sugar	1 L
2 tbsp	flour	30 mL
2 tsp	baking powder	10 mL
1 cup	milk replacement	250 mL
4 tbsp	milk-free margarine	
	touch of salt	
1 tsp	vanilla/maple flavouring	5 mL

Cook together in a double boiler or regular saucepan except for the flavouring, stirring constantly. Boil until the mixture reaches the soft ball stage. Add vanilla and beat until smooth only. Spread in greased pan. Cut into desired pieces after it has set.

Candy/Special Sweet Treats

Frozen Treats

1	pkg milk-free pudding powder (chocolate or any preferred flavour)	1
1/4 cup	sugar	60 mL
3 cups	milk replacement (if using chocolate, vanilla or strawberry use the flavoured milk replacement to add flavour)	750 mL

Mix together and cook over medium heat. Pour into moulds with sticks and freeze.

Alternative method:

1	pkg instant chocolate pudding milk-free	1
2 cups	milk replacement	500 mL
2 cups	vanilla (milk-free) frozen dessert	500 mL

Measure into bowl, mix well with mixer. Pour into moulds with sticks and freeze.

Candy/Special Sweet Treats

Marshmallow Shapes

2	pkgs unflavoured gelatin dissolved in 1/2 cup (125 mL) cold water	2
2 cups	sugar	500 mL
3/4 cup	water	175 mL
1/2 tsp	salt	2 mL
1/2 tsp	vanilla	2 mL

Boil sugar, water and salt until thread stage. Add gelatin and heat until thick and can stand in peaks. Add vanilla and beat for about 20 minutes. Use whatever shape you want for moulds. Fill with marshmallow filling and let sit. Dip into chocolate coating and add a stick to make another kind of treat.

* These can replace the ones on sticks sold in stores. Candy making suppliers have many moulds and the sticks.

Chocolate Coating

1/2 lb	milk-free sweetened dark chocolate	250 g

Melt above in double boiler. Dip shapes once they are cooled and set.

* I have bought chocolate from professional chocolate makers which has never been opened or contaminated by other allergens. Dark chocolate must be used if a milk allergy is present.

Candy/Special Sweet Treats

Candy Apples

6	crisp medium apples	6
6	clean wooden skewers	6
1 1/3 cup	granulated sugar	325 mL
2 cup	corn syrup	500 mL
1/4 tsp	red food colouring	1 mL
10	drops oil of cinnamon (optional)	10

Wash and dry apples. Remove stems. Insert skewers into blossom end.

Combine sugar, syrup and colouring in double boiler. Cook stirring well until sugar dissolves. Cover and cook approximately 8 minutes. Uncover and cook without stirring to hard crack stage. Stir in flavouring if using.

Turn each apple in syrup to coat, twirl to coat evenly. Sprinkle with sugar if you like. Set on greased cookie sheet or greased wax paper.

Candy/Special Sweet Treats

Cereal and Pretzel Snack   250°

1/2 cup	milk-free margarine or oil or 1/2 and 1/2	125 mL
4 tsp	Worcestershire sauce	20 mL
1/2 tsp	celery salt	2 mL
1 tsp	garlic powder	5 mL
1 tsp	paprika	5 mL
3–4 tbsp	honey	45–60 mL
2 tsp	chili powder	10 mL
2 cups	toasted oat cereal of your choice	500 mL
2 cups	whole wheat cereal of your choice	500 mL
3 cups	pretzels	750 mL
2 cups	sweet cereal of your choice	500 mL

Stir together all ingredients except cereals over medium heat. Mix cereals together, pour hot mixture over top and stir well. Place in roaster and bake at 250°F (120°C) for 4–5 hours stirring often.

This recipe can be modified to accommodate taste by increasing amounts of spices or sweetness. This can be frozen in bags after cooling

Fruit Sherbet

1 cup	white sugar	250 mL
1 cup	water (milk replacement can be used, this makes it more creamy)	250 mL
3 1/2 cups	frozen unsweetened fruit	875 mL
2 tbsp	lemon juice	30 mL
1 tbsp	liqueur (optional)	15 mL

Combine sugar and water in saucepan. Heat, stirring until sugar dissolves. Increase heat and simmer for 5 minutes. Set aside to cool. Puree fruit. Blend puree, cooled syrup, lemon juice and liqueur. Mix very well. Freeze mixture in pail or large cake pan. Freeze until almost solid. When the mixture is firm break into pieces and transfer to chilled bowl. Beat until smooth. Store in an airtight container. This makes approximately 4 cups (1L).

Candy/Special Sweet Treats

Caramel Fried Ice Cream   Deep Fry 355°

1 quart	vanilla flavoured frozen milk-free dessert	1 L
1/4 cup	whipped topping - not whipped	60 mL
2 tsp	vanilla	10 mL
2 cups	coconut flakes finely chopped	500 mL
2 cups	finely crushed corn flake cereal	500 mL
1/2 tsp	cinnamon (optional)	2 mL
	cooking oil for deep frying (optional)	
	plastic disposable gloves or plastic wrap	

Caramel Sauce

1 cup	brown sugar	250 mL
1/2 cup	milk-free margarine	125 mL
1/2 cup	milk replacement vanilla	125 mL

Place 8 scoops of frozen dessert on baking sheet. Cover and freeze until very firm. In bowl combine whipped topping and vanilla. In another bowl combine coconut, corn flakes and cinnamon. Remove ice cream from freezer, wearing plastic gloves to shape into balls, dip first into whipped topping, then into coconut mixture, make sure to coat entire surface. Cover and freeze another 3 hours.

For caramel sauce, heat sugar in heavy saucepan over medium heat until partially melted and golden. Add margarine, gradually add milk replacement stirring constantly. Cook and stir for 8 minutes or until sauce is thick and golden. Keep warm over very low heat.

Heat oil in electric skillet or deep fryer to 355°F (175°C). Fry ice cream balls until golden, about 15–30 seconds. Drain on paper towels and serve immediately.

Candy/Special Sweet Treats

Chocolate Pretzels   400°

2	squares unsweetened chocolate	2
1/2 cup	milk-free margarine	125 mL
1/2 cup	sugar	125 mL
1/4 cup	milk replacement (or 1 egg)	60 mL
2 cups	flour	500 mL
1 tsp	vanilla	5 mL
1/4 tsp	salt	1 mL

Melt chocolate and cool. Cream margarine and sugar, add applesauce (or egg) and melted chocolate. Stir in flour, vanilla and salt. Cover and chill. Grease cookie sheets or use non-stick. Divide batter into 12 parts. Pull into ropes 6 inches (15 cm) long. Form into a pretzel shape or any shape you desire. Bake at 400°F (200°C) for 7–9 minutes until firm—cool. Move on to next step.

Glaze for Pretzels

1 cup	milk-free chocolate chips	250 mL
1 tsp	syrup	5 mL
1 tsp	milk-free margarine	5 mL
1 cup	powdered sugar	250 mL
3–5 tbsp	strong hot coffee (optional)	45–75 mL
	- can use any flavour or none at all	

Combine chips, syrup and margarine in saucepan, stir over low heat until melted. Stir in powdered sugar and coffee. Dip pretzels until completely covered. Place on wax paper until set.

Candy/Special Sweet Treats

Old Fashioned Fudge

4 cups	white sugar	1 L
1 cup	milk replacement	250 mL
1 cup	milk-free margarine	250 mL
3/4 cup	cocoa	175 mL
2 cups	flour	500 mL
1–2 tsp	vanilla	5–10 mL

Use heavy pot to cook this. Place sugar, milk and margarine together and bring to a boil with burner on high—watch very closely and stir. Once ingredients are combined remove from heat and do not stir for 10 minutes. Add vanilla and quickly stir in cocoa and flour. Pour into greased pan. Work quickly or fudge will harden.

Chocolate Syrup

1/2 cup	cocoa	125 mL
1 cup	water	250 mL
2 cups	sugar	500 mL
1/8 tsp	salt	1 mL
1/2 tsp	vanilla	2 mL
1 tbsp	milk-free margarine	15 mL

Bring cocoa, water and sugar to boil. Add salt, vanilla and margarine.

Candy/Special Sweet Treats

Hot Fudge Sauce

1/4 cup	cocoa	60 mL
1/2 cup	corn syrup	125 mL
1/2 cup	sugar	125 mL
1/4 cup	milk replacement	60 mL
1/8 tsp	salt	0.5 mL
1 1/2 tbsp	milk-free margarine	22 mL
1/2 tsp	vanilla	2 mL

Combine cocoa, sugar, syrup, milk replacement and margarine and cook over medium heat until mixture comes to a boil. Boil for 3–4 minutes, remove from heat and add vanilla.

Hot Chocolate

There are some safe syrups on the market; otherwise this recipe works well.

1/3–1/2 cup	brown sugar	75–125 mL
2–3 tbsp	cocoa	30–45 mL
1/4 cup	milk replacement	60 mL
3 tbsp	cane syrup	45 mL
2 1/2–3 cups	milk replacement	625–750 mL

Stir together first 4 ingredients over medium heat until smooth. Add 2 1/2–3 cups (625–750 mL) of milk replacement. Serve with marshmallows or whipped topping with cocoa added.

Candy/Special Sweet Treats

Popsicles

1	package jelly dessert powder	1
1	package same flavoured drink mix (unsweetened)	1
2/3 cup	boiling water	150 mL
2 cups	cold water	500 mL
1 cup	sugar	250 mL

Stir together jelly powder, drink mix, sugar and hot water. Stir until dissolved. Add cold water. Stir well. Pour into moulds and freeze.

This can be mixed in a pitcher or measuring cup so pouring into moulds is made easier and less messy.

chapter 7

Main Dishes

✤ *beef*   ✤ *pork*
✤ *chicken/poultry*

Meat and poultry dishes are not as tricky as baking but they do come with their own challenges. Very limited use of sauces, canned soups and other ingredients which often make a recipe go further can present difficulty. Delicious meals can be made with the use of spices and a liberal sprinkling of creativity.

Main - *beef*

Tacos

1	package of hard tacos or soft - milk/egg free	1
1 1/2 lbs	ground lean beef	750 g
1	can tomato soup or tomato sauce	1
1/4 cup	ketchup (optional)	60 mL
	onion to taste	
	salt	
	pepper	
	chili pepper	
	garlic	
	any spices you enjoy	
1/4–1/2 cup	chicken broth	60–125 mL

Pan fry burger in chicken broth in a large frying pan or electric frying pan with onion and spices. Drain fat if necessary. Add tomato soup/tomato sauce (or combination of both) and ketchup. Add chili to taste, keep on low until ready to serve. Meat mixture should not be runny as it will be difficult to fill tacos.

To fill taco:

You can use diced tomatoes, shredded lettuce, refried beans or rice.

Main - *beef*

Chili

1 1/2 lbs	lean ground beef	750 g
1	can tomato soup or tomato sauce (or both)	1
1	small can of tomato paste	1
	onions	
1	can pork and beans (optional)	1
1	can kidney beans (optional)	1
1/8 cup	ketchup	30 mL
2 tbsp	brown sugar	30 mL
1/4–1/2 tsp	dry mustard	1–2 mL
	garlic - fresh or dry	
	chili powder to taste	
	cayenne pepper (optional)	
1/4–1/2 cup	chicken broth	60–125 mL

Brown ground beef in chicken broth and drain if necessary. Add onions and garlic and cook until clear. Add all other ingredients and simmer until time to serve. The longer chili cooks the more flavour it has. Chili has an individual taste so spice it according to your family. Serve with warm garlic bread, rice, salads.

Main - *beef*

Meat Loaf　　　　　　　　　　　　　　　　　　　**350°**

1 lb	lean ground beef	500 g
1/4 tsp	parsley	1 mL
1/4 tsp	dill	1 mL
1/4 tsp	salt	1 mL
1/4 tsp	pepper	1 mL
1/2 cup	rolled oats (optional)	125 mL
1	medium onion diced or use dried onion	1
1/4 cup	ketchup	60 mL
2 tbsp	relish - your choice	30 mL
2 tbsp	mustard	30 mL
	(1 egg)	

Topping

1/4 cup	ketchup	60 mL
4 tbsp	brown sugar	60 mL
1/2 tsp	dry mustard	2 mL
	garlic	
	salt	
	pepper	

Mix together well, put into a greased loaf pan. Spread topping over mixture. Bake at 350°F (180°C) for about an hour.

Main - beef

Meat Loaf 350°

1 1/2 lbs	lean ground beef	750 g
1	pkg onion soup mix	1
3/4 cup	rolled oats	175 mL
2 cups	chopped ham - chopped tiny	500 mL
1/2 cup	ketchup	125 mL
2 tbsp	brown sugar	30 mL
1/2 tsp	mustard	2 mL
2 tsp	soy sauce	10 mL

Mix hamburger with soup mix and rolled oats. Divide into 2 parts. Press one portion into a loaf pan, add ham and cover with other portion. Mix together rest of ingredients and spread over top of loaf. Bake at 350°F (180°C) for 1 to 1 1/2 hours.

Sweet and Sour Meat Balls 350°

1 1/2 lbs	lean ground beef	750 g
1/2 cup	water - or pineapple juice	125 mL
1/2 cup	brown sugar	125 mL
1 tbsp	soy sauce (or more)	15 mL
1/4 cup	vinegar	60 mL
1/4 cup	ketchup	60 mL
	pineapple can be used if desired	
1/4–1/2 cup	chicken broth	60–125 mL

Mix hamburger and roll into small meat balls. Brown in chicken broth in a frying pan. Remove and add to baking dish. Pour sauce over and bake covered at 350°F (180°C) for 1 hour.

The Egg, Dairy & Nut FREE cookbook by Donna Beckwith

Main - *beef*

Spaghetti and Meatballs

Prepare lean hamburger and make into small meatballs. Fry until done.

Prepare spaghetti sauce as follows or use prepared sauce (check closely as many contain cheese).

2	cans tomato soup or 2 cans tomato sauce	2
3	cans tomato paste	3
	salt	
	pepper	
	garlic	
	dried onion or fresh	
	carrots diced or pureed	
	celery	
	oregano (optional)	

Sauté onion and celery (and carrot if you like) add remaining ingredients and simmer for as long as you like.

If making meat sauce crumble lean ground beef and add to tomato sauce. Again simmer for a long as you like to add flavour. Freeze and use as you like.

Main - beef

Meat & Rice Cabbage Rolls   350°

2 lbs	lean beef	1 kg
1 cup	uncooked rice	250 mL
	onion	
	salt	
	pepper	
	garlic	
1–2	cans tomato juice	1–2
1–2	heads of medium cabbage*	1–2

* remove core and soften in boiling water for approximately 10-15 minutes

Mix uncooked beef, rice, onion and spices.

Peel cabbage leaves gently. Put small amount of beef mixture into center of leaf and roll tucking in ends if possible. Layer in baking dish, cover with tomato juice. Bake at 350°F (180°C) for approximately 2 hours. These freeze well.

Main - beef

Hamburger & Chips Casserole   350°

1 lb	lean ground beef	500 g
1/4 cup	chopped pepper (optional)	60 mL
2 tbsp	Worcestershire sauce	30 mL
	(2 eggs)	
1 cup	crushed potato chips (or more)	250 mL
1/4 cup	chopped onion	60 mL
	salt	
	pepper	
1/2 cup	bread crumbs	125 mL
1 can	beef consommé	1

Mix all ingredients except chips. Press into greased baking dish. Sprinkled crushed potato chips on top. Bake at 350°F (180°C) for 1 hour.

Layered Casserole   350°

	layer dish with sliced onions	
1 inch	layer of sliced raw potatoes	2.5 cm
1/2 cup	uncooked long grain rice	125 mL
1	large can of peas with juice	1
	thick layer of thinly sliced carrots	
1 1/2 lbs	lean ground beef	750 g
1	can tomato soup	1

Layer in large casserole as listed. Cover lightly and bake at 350°F (180°C) for 2 1/2 hours.

Main - *beef*

Stew   350°

3 lbs	stew meat well trimmed rolled in spiced flour mixture and browned in oil	1.5 kg
8	potatoes cubed	8
2	onions diced	2
8	carrots - bite size pieces	8
	salt	
	pepper	
	garlic	
	bay leaf (optional)	
1/2	turnip - bite size pieces	1/2
1 1/2 cup	beef stock	375 mL

Put altogether in deep roaster and add water and stock to cover. Cover and bake in oven at 350°F (180°C) for 3–4 hours. Thicken with flour and water mixture prior to serving.

Main - *beef*

Marinated Steak   Broil/BBQ

1 1/2–2 lbs	sirloin steak	750–1000 g

Marinade

1/4 cup	Worcestershire sauce	60 mL
2 tbsp	lemon juice	30 mL
2 tbsp	oil	30 mL
1/4 cup	minced onion	60 mL
3/4 tsp	salt	3 mL
2–3	cloves of garlic	2–3

Sauce

2 tbsp	milk-free margarine	30 mL
1/2 lb	sliced or quartered fresh mushrooms	250 g
1 tbsp	chopped parsley	15 mL
1 tsp	Worcestershire sauce	5 mL

Marinate steak for 3–6 hours turning every hour. Broil on BBQ, 7–10 minutes on each side, brushing occasionally with marinade.

While steak is cooking sauté mushrooms in margarine for 5 minutes over high heat. Reduce heat and add parsley and Worcestershire sauce.

Top steak with sauce and serve.

Main - beef

Pepper Steak

2 lbs	round or sirloin steak cut into strips	1 kg
1/4 cup	vegetable oil	60 mL
1 cup	water or beef broth	250 mL
1	medium onion sliced	1
1/2 tsp	garlic	2 mL
1/4 tsp	ginger	1 mL
2	medium green/red peppers	2
1 tbsp	cornstarch	15 mL
3 tsp	sugar	15 mL
3 tbsp	soy sauce	45 mL
2	medium tomatoes cubed with seeds removed	2

Heat oil in large pan, add meat and cook. Turn frequently. Stir in water/beef broth, onion, garlic and ginger. Heat through. Reduce heat and simmer for 12 minutes or until tender. Add peppers during last 5 minutes. Blend cornstarch, sugar and soy sauce together and add to meat mixture stirring constantly until mixture thickens and boils 1 minute. Place tomatoes on meat mixture and cook on low heat until tomatoes are heated through. Serve with rice.

BBQ Beef in a Slow Cooker

1 cup	ketchup	250 mL
1 cup	BBQ sauce (your choice)	250 mL
1 tsp	chili powder	5 mL
1 tsp	salt	5 mL
2 tbsp	vinegar	30 mL
2 tbsp	brown sugar	30 mL
2 tbsp	Worcestershire sauce	30 mL
2 lbs	stew meat	1 kg

Combine all ingredients in slow cooker. Cook on high 4–6 hours.

Main - *beef*

Steak Strips on Pasta or Rice

1 1/2 lbs	lean round steak cut in strips	750 g
4 tbsp	milk-free margarine	60 mL
1	10 oz (285 g) can mushrooms or fresh	1
1 cup	chopped onion	250 mL
2 cups	chili sauce	500 mL
2 tbsp	flour	30 mL
1/2 cup	cold water	125 mL
1 1/2 cup	frozen green beans	375 mL

Heat skillet and add 3 tbsp (45 mL) margarine. Sauté mushrooms and onions until tender. Remove. Add remaining margarine; add steak and sauté for 5–7 minutes. Add chili sauce. Simmer covered for 10 minutes or until meat is tender. Blend flour with cold water and stir into mixture, bring to a boil. Reduce heat, return mushrooms and onion, add green beans, mix well. Do not boil again but bring to serving temperature. Serve on egg free pasta or rice.

Marinated Beef — Broil/BBQ

1 1/2 lbs	London broil	750 g

Marinade

1/2 cup	soy sauce	125 mL
2 tbsp	brown sugar	30 mL
3 tsp	minced garlic	15 mL
3 tbsp	lemon juice	45 mL
1 1/2 tbsp	olive oil	23 mL
1 cup	beef bouillon	250 mL
	spice	

Mix together ingredients and place beef into a shallow baking dish. Pour sauce over, reserve 1/3 of sauce. Cover and refrigerate overnight. Place meat on broiler, baste with remaining marinade. Slice diagonally across the grain—serve.

Main - *beef*

Rolled Steak 350°

1 1/2 lbs	round steak (tenderized)	750 g
3 tbsp	milk-free margarine	45 mL
1/4 cup	chopped onion	60 mL
2 cups	bread crumbs	500 mL
1/2 cup	chopped celery	125 mL
1/2 tsp	salt	2 mL
1/4 tsp	sage	1 mL
	pepper	
1 tbsp	water	15 mL
	bacon strips	

Lightly fry onion and celery in margarine, add bread crumbs and water. Place dressing on steak, roll up and then wrap bacon around each piece of steak. Fasten with metal picks. Roll in flour and brown in hot oil. Place in casserole dish, season more and bake 1 hour at 350°F (180°C).

* Instead of a casserole dish you can wrap each piece in foil prior to baking.

Main - *pork*

Pork Cutlets

**pork cutlets
flour
garlic
salt
pepper
small amount of cornmeal
oil
spice to taste**

Mix flour and other dry ingredients in bag or in dish. Cover each piece of meat and add to hot oil in frying pan. Turn as required. Cutlets should be nice and crunchy.

Main - pork

BBQ Spareribs   350°

* this sauce is also good on chicken and beef ribs

4–5 lbs	spare ribs	2–2.5 kg
1 1/2 cup	ketchup	375 mL
1	small can tomato paste	1
1 cup	water or juice (apple/pineapple)	250 mL
1 tsp	chili powder	5 mL
2 tbsp	Worcestershire sauce	30 mL
4 tbsp	vinegar	60 mL
4 tbsp	brown sugar	60 mL
	salt	
	pepper	
1 tbsp	dry mustard	15 mL
	onion - dried or diced	

** *Approximately 4–5 lbs spare ribs trimmed that have been simmered for at least 1–2 hours on stove or in oven with onion and salt and pepper (this removes a lot of the fat).*

Mix these ingredients and pour over pre-cooked ribs. Cook covered at 350°F (180°C) for 2 hours. Serve with rice and salad. Sauce is good on rice.

Main - *pork*

Sausage Casserole 350°

2 cups	sauerkraut	500 mL
1	can applesauce or 5–6 cut up apples	1
1/2 cup	dry wine	125 mL
2 tbsp	brown sugar	30 mL
2–3	cooked onions	2–3
9–10	sausages of choice	9–10
2 cups	potatoes (boiled)	500 mL

Combine all ingredients in roaster. Cook at 350°F (180°C) for approximately 1–2 hours. Serve hot.

Sauce for Pork or Chicken

1/2 cup	crabapple jelly	125 mL
1/2 cup	ketchup	125 mL
1 tbsp	vinegar	15 mL
1/2 tsp	chili	2 mL
1/2 tsp	salt	2 mL
1/2 tsp	garlic	2 mL

Increase spices to your taste. Mix all ingredients and simmer for 2 minutes. Pour over pork or chicken when ready to serve or pour over raw pork or chicken and bake in oven until done.

This sauce can be used for grilled or roasted meat.

Main - *pork*

Pork Kabobs   BBQ

	juice of 1 lime	
1/4 cup	oil	60 mL
1/4 tsp	crushed coriander	1 mL
1/4 cup	chopped onion	60 mL
2	cloves crushed garlic	2
1/4–1/2 tsp	pepper	1–2 mL
	salt	
2 lbs	pork cut into cubes	1 kg

Marinate pork in sauce overnight, put onto soaked wooden skewers or metal skewers and grill on BBQ.

Main - pork

Roast Pork with Garlic and Rosemary   350°

4–5 lb	roast	2–2.5 kg
3	cloves of garlic crushed	3
1 tbsp	chopped fresh rosemary	15 mL
1 tbsp	salt	15 mL
2 tbsp	olive oil	30 mL
3	bay leaves	3
1 cup	water	250 mL
1/3 cup	red wine vinegar	75 mL

Combine garlic, rosemary, salt and oil and mix well. Rub this mixture over pork. Place on rack in a baking dish, add bay leaves and water and vinegar to dish. Bake at 350°F (180°C) for 1 1/2–2 hours. Remove from baking dish and wrap in foil for 15 minutes prior to serving.

Hawaiian Style Spareribs   350°

2	sides of spareribs - pre-boiled and cut into serving pieces	2

Sauce

2 tbsp	brown sugar	30 mL
2 tbsp	cornstarch	30 mL
1/2 tsp	salt	2 mL
1/2 cup	vinegar	125 mL
1/2 cup	ketchup	125 mL
1	can crushed pineapple - not drained	1
1 tbsp	soy sauce	15 mL

Combine sugar, cornstarch and salt, stir in vinegar and ketchup and crushed pineapple and soy sauce. Cook this mixture until slightly thickened. Arrange ribs in roasting pan and cover with sauce. Bake at 350°F (180°C) for 1 1/2–2 hours.

Main - pork

Bacon Wrapped Pork Roast 375°

1	pork loin roast - approximately 2–3 lbs (1–1.5 kg)	1
	salt	
	pepper	
1 tbsp	olive oil	15 mL
2 1/2 tsp	fresh rosemary or dried	12 mL
1	pkg of favourite bacon	1
3	small onions peeled	3

Season meat with salt and pepper. Heat oil in pan sear meat on all sides. Rub meat with rosemary and wrap with bacon. Roast in oven at 375°F (190°C) until juice runs clear. Baste roast regularly to enhance taste.

Ribs with Hot Sauce Broil/BBQ

Back ribs - trimmed and cleaned
hot sauce of choice

Place ribs on broiler pan, brush with hot sauce. Broil and turn over, repeat with hot sauce. Cut into pieces and serve.

Main - *chicken/poultry*

Spicy Chicken Wings   400°

3 lbs	chicken wings tip removed	1.5 kg
3	cloves of garlic	3
1 tbsp	ground coriander	15 mL
1 tsp	dried cumin	5 mL
1/2 tsp	hot pepper flakes	2 mL
2 tbsp	oil	30 mL
2 tbsp	vinegar	30 mL
1 tbsp	soy sauce	15 mL

Combine spices, stir in oil and vinegar and soy sauce. Toss wings until well covered. Marinate in fridge for 4 hours or overnight. Bake or broil on greased pan at 400°F (200°C) until meat easily comes away from the bone (approximately 45 minutes). If baking, broil at end to make crispy.

Hot Wings   400°

Broiled version - remove tip and separate wing parts. Toss chicken wings in your favourite hot pepper sauce (no sugar added). Put on broiler. Turn and coat again with hot sauce.

Deep Fried version - lightly toss cut chicken wings in flour, deep fry in hot oil. Toss in hot sauce and serve.

Main - *chicken/poultry*

Smothered Chicken 350°

	chicken pieces	
	crushed soda crackers or flour	
	to coat chicken	
1/2 cup	chopped onion	125 mL
1/2 lb	fresh mushrooms or 1 can	250 g
3 tbsp	sherry (optional)	45 mL
1/2 cup	oil/milk-free margarine or chicken fat	125 mL
6 tbsp	flour	90 mL
3 cups	milk replacement	750 mL
	salt	
	pepper	
2–4	cloves of garlic	2–4
2	stalks of celery minced	2

Coat chicken pieces with crushed soda cracker crumbs or flour. Heat oil and add pieces until browned. Remove browned chicken and put into casserole dish. To remaining oil add onion, garlic and celery, cook until soft. Stir in flour. Slowly add milk replacement and stir over low heat until thick and smooth. Season to taste. Pour gravy over chicken. Cover and bake at 350°F (180°C) for approximately 1 to 1 1/2 hours.

Main - *chicken/poultry*

Ginger Chicken/Turkey Kabobs — BBQ

1–2 lbs	boneless, skinless turkey/chicken breast cut into kabobs	500–1000 g

Combine all the following ingredients into a sealed bag or leak proof container.

1/2 cup	berry jelly or jam	125 mL
1/4 cup	soy sauce	60 mL
2 tbsp	grated ginger	30 mL
2 tbsp	lemon juice	30 mL
3	cloves of garlic crushed	3
	*if you enjoy more spice increase amounts and add others such as cayenne	
1/4 cup	oil	60 mL

Add turkey pieces and marinate for 3–24 hours in fridge. Place turkey on pre-soaked skewers and grill 5–10 minutes over medium heat on the BBQ—turning occasionally.

Garlic Chicken — Broil

3 lbs	chicken cut up	1500 g
1/2 cup	milk-free margarine softened	125 mL
4	cloves garlic minced	4
1 tsp	dried parsley	5 mL
1/4 tsp	dried rosemary	1 mL
1/4 tsp	dried thyme	1 mL

Mix the margarine and spices a day ahead to enhance taste. Place chicken on broiler pan, spread tops of pieces evenly with small amounts of mixture. Broil chicken, turning and coating frequently until done—approximately 40 minutes to 1 hour.

Main - *chicken/poultry*

Chicken Fingers

	oil	
2 lbs	chicken or turkey breast	1 kg
	cut into strips or cubes	
1 1/2 cup	flour	375 mL
1 tsp	salt	5 mL
1 tsp	pepper	5 mL
1/2 tsp	garlic	2 mL
1/4 cup	cornmeal	60 mL
	spices you enjoy	

Combine flour, cornmeal and spices in a sealed bag. Add chicken/turkey pieces to coat. Heat oil in large frying pan and add pieces. Cook uncovered turning once.

Chicken and Noodles

	vegetable oil	
1 tbsp	vegetable oil	15 mL
4	skinless/boneless chicken/turkey breast	4
10 oz	can chicken broth	285 g
3/4 cup	water	175 mL
1/2 tsp	basil leaves crushed	2 mL
1/4 tsp	pepper	1 mL
2	pkg chicken flavour instant noodles	2
10 oz	pkg frozen peas or pearl onions	285 g
1/4 tsp	paprika	1 mL

Heat oil and add chicken, cook until almost done—remove and set aside. In another pan combine broth, water, spices, heat to boiling. Return chicken to pan, add noodles and peas. Return to boiling. Reduce heat, cover and cook for 10 minutes. Sprinkle paprika over chicken prior to serving.

Main - *chicken/poultry*

Honey Curry Chicken — 350°

1	chicken cut up or pieces of your choice	1
2/3 cup	milk-free margarine melted	150 mL
1 cup	honey	250 mL
1/2 cup	mustard	125 mL
2 tbsp	stronger mustard - Dijon for example	30 mL
8 tsp	curry powder	40 mL

Mix well and pour over chicken. This can be done in a skillet or electric frying pan. In this case meat will have to be turned. If using a cooking dish simply pour over chicken, cover and bake at 350°F (180°C) for approximately 1 hour.

Dijon Sauce — BBQ

1/4 cup	vegetable oil	60 mL
1/4 cup	honey	60 mL
2 tbsp	Dijon mustard	30 mL
1	clove garlic	1
1/4 tsp	dried thyme	1 mL
	salt to taste	
	pepper to taste	

Turkey or chicken pieces can be marinated and then cooked in sauce or simply brush on sauce and grill over medium heat. Watch carefully as the honey will burn quickly.

Main - *chicken/poultry*

Chicken or Turkey Tacos

1 1/2 lbs	ground turkey	750 g
1	small onion minced	1
1 tbsp	oil	15 mL
1/2 tsp	oregano	2 mL
1–2 tbsp	chili	15–30 mL
	salt	
	pepper	
1/2 tsp	garlic	2 mL
	taco shells	
1/4–1/2 cup	chicken broth	60–125 mL

Sauté above in chicken broth until meat is cooked. Do not over cook as it will be dry. Spoon into taco shells—serve with tomatoes, guacamole and salsa.

Turkey or Chicken Burgers   BBQ/GRILL

1 1/2 lbs	ground turkey or chicken	750 g
1/4 cup	minced onion	60 mL
1/2 cup	BBQ sauce	125 mL
1/2 cup	dried breadcrumbs - milk/egg-free	125 mL
	salt to taste	
	pepper to taste	
	spice to taste	

Combine all above and mix well. Shape into patties, place on oiled grill until no longer pink inside. Baste towards the end of grilling with favourite grilling sauce.

Main - *chicken/poultry*

Chicken or Turkey Marinara

2	green or red peppers	2
1	large carrot	1
1	zucchini	1
1 tbsp	olive oil	15 mL
4	skinless/boneless breasts or equivalent turkey pounded to 1/4 inch (0.5 cm) thickness	4
1/2 tsp	dried oregano	2 mL
	salt	
	pepper	
14 oz	can stew tomatoes	400 g
3/4 cup	sliced black olives	175 mL
8–10	sliced mushrooms	8–10

Cut all vegetables into strips or bite size pieces. Cook chicken in oil until lightly brown, approximately 4 minutes per side. Sprinkle with spices.

Remove chicken; add tomatoes, olives, mushrooms, peppers, carrot and zucchini, and cook covered for 3 minutes. Return chicken and increase heat to medium/high. Cook uncovered for about 7–8 more minutes. Sauce should slightly thicken, vegetables should just be tender.

Main - chicken/poultry

Sweet and Sour Chicken   375°

12 tbsp	oil	180 mL
14 tbsp	soy sauce	210 mL
12 tbsp	honey	180 mL
6 tbsp	vinegar	90 mL
3 tsp	thyme	15 mL
3 tsp	paprika	15 mL
1 1/2 tsp	cayenne	7 mL
2 tsp	pepper	10 mL
8	chicken breasts	8

Mix ingredients together to make sauce. Pour into shallow baking dish. Pierce each side of breast with a fork. Place in sauce and coat well. Bake at 375°F (190°C) basting chicken several times for 30–40 minutes.

Spicy Broiled Chicken   Broil/BBQ

1–3 lbs	chicken quartered	500–1500 g
2 tbsp	spice mix (prepared or make your own*)	30 mL
2 tbsp	vegetable oil	30 mL

Shake spice and oil together. Brush on chicken coating well. Broil chicken, turning twice and put any remaining sauce on chicken during cooking time.

* Spice Mix for broiled chicken

1/4 cup	garlic powder	60 mL
2 tbsp	ground cumin	30 mL
2 tbsp	paprika	30 mL
2 tbsp	seasoning salt	30 mL
2 tbsp	pepper	30 mL
2 tbsp	lemon pepper	30 mL
1 tbsp	cayenne	15 mL

Main - *chicken/poultry*

Curry Chicken with Coconut

4	skinless/boneless chicken/turkey breast cut into cubes	4
2 tbsp	vegetable oil	30 mL
1	large onion - chopped	1
4	garlic cloves - finely minced	4
2	whole cloves	2
1 1/2 tbsp	finely grated ginger	23 mL
2 tsp	ground cumin	10 mL
2–3 tsp	chili powder	10–15 mL
1–2 tsp	salt	5–10 mL
1 tsp	ground turmeric	5 mL
1/2 tsp	ground cardamom	2 mL
1/2–3/4 tsp	mustard powder	2–3 mL
1	can unsweetened coconut milk	1
1/2 cup	water	125 mL
1 cup	coarsely chopped coriander	250 mL
3–4 tsp	fresh squeezed lemon juice	15–20 mL

Heat oil in saucepan, add whole cloves to pan and stir-fry until fragrant. Add onion and garlic. Cook until onion softens. Increase heat and add chicken. Stir-fry until chicken is lightly browned. Stir in spices and then coconut milk and water. Cover and reduce heat to medium. Simmer stirring often—approximately 30 minutes. Add lemon juice. Serve immediately.

Main - chicken/poultry

Cornish Hens with Wild Rice 350°

This is a nice dish for special occasions.

4	Cornish hens - less or more depending upon servings - adjust recipe as required	4
4	garlic cloves	4
	salt	
	pepper	
	red currant jelly - heated to liquid	
	red wine - to taste	

Heat together jelly and wine. Place hens in open shallow baking dish. Place one clove of garlic in each hen. Baste each hen with jelly. Continue basting each hen throughout roasting every 20 minutes. Roasting time approximately 1 to 1 1/2 hours at 350°F (180°C). Place hens with legs together and garnish around hens with oven fried rice or packaged wild rice.

Stuffing for Chicken or Turkey

	white or whole wheat bread cut into small pieces - milk and egg free	
1/4–1/2 cup	milk-free margarine	60–125 mL
1–2	medium onions chopped finely	1–2
	poultry seasoning of choice	
	salt	
	pepper	

Sauté chopped onion in 1/4–1/2 cup milk-free margarine until soft. Add salt. Pour over bread and mix well. Put into chicken or turkey. If cooking outside bird put into well greased tinfoil.

Main - *chicken/poultry*

Oven Fried Rice   350°

1 1/2 cups	diced chicken	375 mL
4 cups	water	1 L
2 cups	rice	500 mL
1/2 cup	oil	125 mL
1	can mushrooms - drained	1
1	pkg onion soup mix	1
1/4 cup	soy sauce	60 mL

Combine all ingredients and bake at 350°F (180°C) for 1 hour.

* 2 cups of chicken broth and 2 cups of water can also be used for more flavour.

Oven Fried Chicken   350°

1	chicken cut up	1
1 cup	flour	250 mL
1 tsp	salt	5 mL
1/2 tsp	pepper	2 mL
1 tsp	paprika	5 mL
	add any spices you like	

Mix flour and spices together in a bag. Shake pieces of chicken in flour. Place on baking sheets for 20–30 minutes at 450°F (230°C). Following this, place chicken pieces in roaster and roast covered at 350°F (180°C) for approximately 1 hour.

chapter 8

Soups

Soups

Pea Soup 300°

1–2	ham bones with some meat left on	1–2
3 cups	well-washed split green peas	750 mL
1	diced onion	1
	salt to taste	
	pepper to taste	
	large roaster	

Place bones, peas and onion in large roaster. Cover with water to 3/4 full. Spice to taste. Cook for 4–6 hours at 300°F (150°C), stirring often. Thin with water if soup is too thick. Remove bone and all small bone pieces which may have come loose during cooking. Leave meat in soup. This soup freezes well.

Bean Soup 300°

16 cups	water	4 L
1	bag white beans - soaked overnight	1
1	large onion	1
1 cup	chopped celery	250 mL
2	chopped carrots	2
2 cups	tomato juice	500 mL
1/4 tsp	sweet basil	1 mL
1/2 tsp	parsley	2 mL
1 tbsp	chicken stock powder	15 mL
	salt to taste	
	pepper to taste	
1	bay leaf	1
1	large hambone with some meat on	1
1–2	cans diced tomatoes	1–2

Put all ingredients in large roaster. Bake for 3–4 hours at 300°F (150°C). This soup freezes well.

Soups

Corn Chowder

3 tbsp	milk-free margarine	45 mL
3 tbsp	flour	45 mL
2 1/2–3 cups	unflavoured milk replacement	625–750 mL
	salt	
	pepper	
2	cans of cream corn	2
2	cans of kernel corn	2
1	small chopped onion - cooked	1
3/4 cup	chicken broth	175 mL
1–2	packages of cooked and crumbled bacon	1–2

Melt margarine and stir in flour to make paste. Slowly stir in milk. Add salt and pepper. Stir in remaining ingredients and cook on low for 1 hour. This soup is even tastier the next day.

Cream of Potato

2 cups	mashed potatoes	500 mL
1 cup	chicken broth	250 mL
1 cup	unflavoured milk replacement	250 mL
1/2 cup	diced cooked or fried onion	125 mL
1/2 cup	cooked bacon	125 mL
	salt	
	pepper	

Stir together mashed potatoes, add milk replacement, chicken broth and remaining ingredients. Cook on low heat for approximately 1 hour to allow flavours to blend.

* Other vegetables can be used such as cauliflower, asparagus or broccoli. Substitute for mashed potatoes and bacon.

Soups

Hamburger Soup   300°

1 lb	ground beef - browned and extra fat removed	450 g
1	medium onion - diced and sautéed	1
1	can tomatoes	1
2 cups	water	500 mL
3	cans beef consommé or home-made broth	3
1	can tomato soup	1
4–6	carrots - chopped to bite size pieces	4–6
1	bay leaf	1
1 tbsp	parsley	15 mL
1 tsp	oregano	5 mL
1 tsp	thyme	5 mL
1 tsp	rosemary	5 mL
3/4 cup	pearl barley	175 mL
	salt to taste	
	pepper to taste	
1/4 cup	Worcestershire sauce	50 mL
	spices are optional - use to your taste	

Put all ingredients into slow cooker and cook for several hours. Or put in roaster and place in oven for 2–3 hours at 300°F (150°C). This soup freezes well.

Soup Broth - Beef Stock

6 lbs	beef bones with meat on	2.75 kg
4	carrots	4
2	stalks of celery	2
1	bay leaf	1
1	large onion cut into four with skins on	1

Place bones and all ingredients into large stock pot. Cook for several hours, strain and cool. Remove any fat from top. Use with vegetables, barley or noodles to make your favourite soup. This soup broth can be frozen to use later.

Soups

Chicken Noodle Soup 350°

> left over chicken meat and
> bone or fresh chicken pieces
> onion
> celery
> carrot
> salt
> pepper
> spice to your taste
> egg free noodles

Place chicken in roaster with all ingredients except noodles. Cover with water. Cook at 350°F (180°C) for 2–3 hours. Strain broth twice to remove any bone pieces. Cool overnight and remove any fat from the top. Add noodles to broth. More vegetables and meat can also be added.

Cream of Chicken Soup

2 cups	chicken broth	500 mL
1 cup	cut up left over chicken	250 mL
	salt	
	pepper	
1	bay leaf	1
1/3 cup	finely chopped onion	75 mL
2–3	cut up potatoes	2–3
3–4 tbsp	milk-free margarine	45–60 mL
3–4 tbsp	flour	45–60 mL
1 cup	milk replacement	250 mL
	diced carrots can also be added	

Melt margarine add onion and cook until onions are transparent, add spices. Stir in flour to make a paste. Slowly add chicken broth and milk replacement. Bring to a boil, add potatoes, cover and simmer until potatoes are soft and ready to serve.

Soups

Minestrone Soup

8 cups	beef broth	2 L
1 cup	navy beans (soaked overnight)	250 mL
2 tbsp	salt	30 mL
2 tsp	pepper	10 mL
1 1/2 cups	finely chopped onion	375 mL
2–3	cloves of garlic minced	2–3
1 1/2 cups	chopped carrot	375 mL
1 cup	chopped celery	250 mL
2 cups	finely chopped cabbage	500 mL
2 tbsp	parsley	30 mL
3–4	cut up potatoes	3–4
1 lb	ground beef (browned)	450 g
1 cup	chopped zucchini	250 mL
1 cup	green beans	250 mL
1 1/2 cups	broken spaghetti	375 mL
	basil to taste	

* Tomatoes are also very good in this recipe

Stir together all ingredients except zucchini, green beans and spaghetti. Simmer until vegetables are soft. Add remaining ingredients, spice to taste and serve.

Soups

Beet/Cabbage Borscht

6–8 cups	beef stock	1.5–2 L
2	tins of canned tomatoes	2
1 cup	sliced cabbage	250 mL
1 cup	diced potatoes	250 mL
1 cup	beets (pre cooked, skinned and shredded)	250 mL
	dill	
1/4 cup	onion	50 mL
	salt	
	pepper	
	juice of a lemon	

Simmer all ingredients together. Serve when vegetables are tender.

Chicken broth and meat can also be used.

Cream of Tomato Soup

2 cups	tomatoes (puréed and seeded) or tomato juice	500 mL
2–3	slices of onion	2–3
2 tsp	sugar	10 mL
4 tbsp	milk-free margarine	60 mL
4 tbsp	flour	60 mL
2 cups	unflavoured milk replacement	500 mL
2 cups	chicken broth	500 mL
	salt to taste	
	pepper to taste	

Melt margarine, blend in flour. Add cold tomatoes or juice, onions, sugar and milk replacement. Heat together until soup thickens, stirring constantly. Season and serve.

Soups

Cream of Carrot Soup

4 cups	carrots cut up	1 L
1 1/2 cups	diced potato	375 mL
4 cups	chicken broth	1 L
1/2 cup	chopped onion	125 mL
3 tbsp	milk-free margarine	45 mL
2 tbsp	flour	30 mL
1 tsp	salt	5 mL
1/2 tsp	pepper	2 mL
2 cups	unflavoured milk replacement	500 mL

Combine carrots potato, broth and onion. Cook until vegetables are soft, do not drain. Cool slightly and blend.

Melt margarine, stir in flour, salt and pepper. Add milk replacement. Bring to a boil and cook until thickened. Add carrot mixture, reheat and serve.

Cooked celery or fried mushrooms can be substituted to make cream of celery or cream of mushroom.

chapter 9

Salads & Sauces

Salads and Sauces

Salsa

1	large bowl of cherry tomatoes - approximately 16–18 cups	1
3	mild chili peppers	3
1	large Spanish onion - minced	1
1	large green pepper - minced	1
1	large red pepper - minced	1
	jalapeno peppers - minced (optional)	
3/4 cup	vinegar	175 mL
1/4 cup	brown sugar	60 mL
1 tbsp	course pickling salt	15 mL
2 tsp	paprika	10 mL
2 tsp	garlic	10 mL

Cook for 5–6 hours over low heat, stirring often. This can be canned or frozen.

Salads and Sauces

Antipasto

4 oz	olive oil	125 g
1	medium cauliflower - minced	1
4	tins black olives - pitted	4
1	16 oz (500 g) jar green salad olives	1
1	16 oz (500 g) jar pickled onions	1
2	cans sliced mushrooms	2
2	large green peppers - chopped and minced	2
2	large red peppers - chopped and minced	2
2	4 oz (125 g) jars pimentos - chopped	2
2	500 ml ketchup	2
1	small hot ketchup	1
1	large jar of mixed pickles - chopped and minced	1
1 cup	red wine	250 mL
2	cans lobster*	2
3	cans crab*	3
3	cans shrimp*	3

Simmer this all together for 1 hour. This can be canned or frozen. Good served with crackers.

imitation can be used with great results. Note: DO NOT USE if egg allergy exists as they contain egg white.

Salads and Sauces

Basic White Sauce

Increase depending on number of servings

Medium

2 tbsp	milk-free margarine	30 mL
2 tbsp	flour	30 mL
1 cup	milk replacement	250 mL
1/4 tsp	salt	1 mL
1/8 tsp	pepper	0.5 mL

Melt margarine and stir in flour in medium size saucepan, stirring constantly. Slowly add milk replacement. Reduce heat and cook 3 minutes. Seasonings of choice can be added, wine in place of some milk replacement.

Reduce margarine to 1 tbsp (15 mL) and 1 tbsp (15 mL) flour for thin white sauce.

Increase margarine to 3 tbsp (45 mL) and 3 tbsp (45 mL) flour for thick sauce.

Pasta Sauces - cream

Use basic white sauce, increase to accommodate servings. Add seasonings and chicken breast, vegetables or seafood. Pour over pasta of choice and toss.

Salads and Sauces

Supreme Salad

Prepare ahead and toss just prior to serving

Dressing

1/8–1/4 cup	salad oil	60 mL
1/4 cup	white sugar	60 mL
3 tbsp	white vinegar or your choice	45 mL
2 2/3 tbsp	ketchup	40 mL
1 tbsp	grated onion	15 mL
1–2 tbsp	Worcestershire sauce	15–30 mL

Mix together and store in covered container at least overnight.

Salad

	large head of Romaine lettuce, washed well and cut into bite size pieces	
5–10	pieces of crumbled bacon	5–10
1 cup	fresh bean sprouts	250 mL

Cooked chicken or other meat or shellfish can be added to this salad just prior to tossing.

Carrot and Raisin Salad

2 cups	shredded carrots	500 mL
3/4 cup	well washed raisins	175 mL
1/3–2/3 cup	soy based mayonnaise (milk & egg free)	75–150 mL
1–2 tbsp	vinegar	15–30 mL
1–2 tbsp	sugar	15–30 mL

Put all ingredients into a bowl—toss together.

The Egg, Dairy & Nut FREE cookbook by Donna Beckwith

Salads and Sauces

Fried Pepper and Beans

2	red peppers sliced	2
2 cups	frozen French style green beans	500 mL
	onion	
2 tbsp	hot sauce	30 mL
	salt	
	pepper	
	garlic	
1–2 tbsp	oil	15–30 mL

Fry gently in large frying pan. A nice variation to everyday beans.

Sweet Potato Casserole 350°

3	baked and peeled large sweet potatoes - mashed	3
1	tin pineapple tidbits - not drained	1
4 tbsp	melted milk-free margarine	60 mL
4 tbsp	brown sugar	60 mL
1 1/2–2 cups	miniature marshmallows	375–500 mL

Drain pineapple and keep juice. Add margarine and sugar to mashed potatoes. Stir in pineapple juice. Add pineapple and marshmallows. Put in greased pan, heat until marshmallows melt—approximately 1/2 hour at 350°F (180°C).

Salads and Sauces

Rice Salad

1 cup	cooked rice	250 mL
1	can crushed pineapple - well drained (optional)	
1/2 cup	white sugar	125 mL
1 cup	milk-free whipped topping - whipped	250 mL
1/4 cup	soy based mayonnaise* lettuce - leaves well washed and dried cherries - dried or drained Maraschino	60 mL

*coconut milk (not light) can be used

Combine rice, pineapple and sugar. Whip topping until stiff, beat in mayonnaise. Fold into rice mixture. Spoon this mixture onto lettuce, top with dried cherries.

Dill Cucumbers

1 cup	sliced cucumbers	250 mL
1/4 cup	milk and egg free mayonnaise dill - to taste	60 mL
1 tbsp	sugar - to taste	15 mL

Mix altogether and serve as dip.

Salads and Sauces

Bean Salad

Dressing

1/4 cup	vinegar	60 mL
1/2 cup	oil	125 mL
1/4 tsp	pepper	1 mL
1/2 tsp	salt	2 mL
1 tsp	dry mustard	5 mL
1 tsp	thyme	5 mL
1/2 tsp	garlic salt or powder	2 mL
1	tin green beans	1
1	tin cut wax beans	1
1	tin kidney beans	1
1	tin lima beans	1
1	tin chick peas	1
1	cup chopped celery	1
1/2 cup	onion chopped or rings	125 mL
1/4 cup	green or red peppers	60 mL

Sprinkle with salt and put dressing over vegetables. Store in airtight container.

Salads and Sauces

Favourite Salad

	medium cabbage shredded	
2 cups	bean sprouts or 1 can	500 mL
2 cups	fresh mushrooms - sliced	500 mL
3	green onions - sliced	3
1/2 cup	sunflower seeds	125 mL
	- check as many have nut warnings	
2	pkgs instant Japanese noodles broken into small pieces	2

Dressing

2	packets of seasoning from noodles (milk-free)	2
1/4 – 1/2 cup	oil	60 – 125 mL
4 – 6 tbsp	soy sauce	60 – 90 mL
6 tbsp	vinegar	90 mL
3 tbsp	sugar	45 mL
	salt	
	pepper	

Mix all ingredients except dressing and noodles.

Mix all ingredients for dressing and set aside until ready to use. Shake well prior to using.

When ready to serve, crumble noodles over salad and add dressing. Toss.

Grilled shrimp or chicken can be added to this recipe as well.

Onions for the BBQ

large purple onions
balsamic vinegar

Large purple onions sliced thickly and marinated in balsamic vinegar. Place on grill, turning a couple of times. These are great with grilled meat.

Salads and Sauces

Greek Lemon Potatoes   475°

3 lbs	potatoes	1.5 kg
1/2 cup	fresh lemon juice	125 mL
1/3 cup	vegetable oil	75 mL
2 tsp	salt	10 mL
1/2 tsp	black pepper	2 mL
1 1/2 tsp	dried oregano	12 mL
2	garlic cloves - crushed	2
3 cups	hot water	750 mL
	fresh parsley to garnish	

Toss together potatoes, lemon juice, oil, spices and garlic in 9x13 inch (22x33 cm) pan. Add hot water. Bake uncovered for 1 1/2 hours at 475°F (240°C), stirring every 20 minutes. Add more hot water if necessary to prevent sticking. Be careful not to let potatoes burn the last 30 minutes. During the last 15–20 minutes, allow the water to evaporate until only the oil is left. Garnish with parsley and serve.

Scalloped Potatoes   350°

6–8	sliced medium potatoes	6–8
2 tbsp	milk-free margarine	30 mL
2 tbsp	flour	30 mL
1/2 tsp	salt	2 mL
	pepper to taste	
2 cups	milk replacement	500 mL
	spices as you like	
	sliced onion (optional)	

Melt 2 tbsp margarine, add flour. Add milk replacement slowly and bring to a boil. Add salt and pepper. Pour over sliced onions and potatoes in large casserole dish. Bake uncovered for 1–1 1/2 hours at 350°F (180°C).

Salads and Sauces

Quick and Easy Potatoes   350°

* amounts vary on how many servings you need 1–2 potatoes per person (adult)

	sliced potatoes	
5 tbsp	milk-free margarine	75 mL
	sliced onion	
	sliced carrots	
3 tbsp	water	45 mL
	season to what you like	

Combine potatoes, onion and carrots in casserole. Top with margarine, water and seasonings. Cook for 1–1 1/2 hours covered at 350°F (180°C).

Fancy Potatoes   400°

6	potatoes peeled and washed	6
2 tbsp	melted milk-free margarine	30 mL
1 tsp	salt	5 mL
2 tbsp	milk-free margarine - second amount	15 mL
1/4 cup	bread crumbs	60 mL

Slice potatoes at 1/8 inch (3 mm) intervals—do not cut through. Arrange potatoes sliced sides up in greased dish. Brush with first amount of margarine. Sprinkle with salt and breadcrumbs. Bake approximately 30–40 minutes at 400°. Sprinkle with remaining margarine. Bake additional 15–20 minutes.

Salads and Sauces

Vegetable Salad

1–2	heads cauliflower	1–2
1–2	baskets cherry tomatoes	1–2
1	bunch broccoli with stems	1
4	carrots cut into small strips	4
1	bunch chopped green onion	1
3	stalks celery	3
2	cans button mushrooms	2
1	8 oz (250 g) bottle Italian dressing	1

Prepare all vegetables cutting into bite size pieces except cherry tomatoes. Put all ingredients into plastic bowl or double plastic bags. Pour dressing over to cover all vegetables. Seal. Marinate overnight or for 24 hours turning frequently. Drain thoroughly before serving.

BBQ Potatoes — 350°

1/4 cup	melted milk-free margarine	60 mL
3 tbsp	ketchup	45 mL
1 tsp	chili powder	5 mL
1 tsp	brown sugar	5 mL
1/8 tsp	salt	0.5 mL
1/8 tsp	pepper	0.5 mL
	potatoes peeled and cut into pieces	

Mix and pour over potatoes.

Bake for 1 1/2 hours at 350°F (180°C).

Salads and Sauces

Oven Potatoes   400°

4–5	medium potatoes - peeled and diced	4–5
1 tbsp	oil	15 mL
1 tbsp	vinegar	15 mL
2	large cloves of garlic crushed	2
1 tsp	dried thyme crumbled	5 mL
1 tsp	dried leaf oregano	5 mL
	salt and pepper	

Brush mixture onto potatoes. Place on baking sheet for 15 minutes at 400°F (200°C). Turn and bake 10–20 minutes longer or until tender.

Crunchy Coated Potatoes   400°

1/4 cup	milk-free margarine - melted	60 mL
3 tbsp	finely chopped onion - sautéed	45 mL
3	large potatoes	3
1–2 cups	crushed corn flakes cereal	250–500 mL
	salt and pepper to taste	

Slice potatoes 1/8 inch thick. Place on greased 9x13 inch (22x33 cm) pan. Pour melted margarine and sautéed onions over potato slices. Sprinkle corn flakes over top and bake for 30 minutes at 400°F (200°C).

Salads and Sauces

Baked Vegetables   325°

8	carrots	8
1	bunch celery	1
1	large onion	1
1	large pepper - your choice	1
2	cans green beans - drained	2
2	cans stewed tomatoes	2
1/2 cup	milk-free margarine	125 mL
1 tbsp	sugar	15 mL
3 tbsp	minute tapioca	45 mL
	salt and pepper	

Cut vegetables into bite size pieces. Add everything together. Cover and bake for 2 hours at 325°F (160°C). Do not use cauliflower or broccoli as they become too mushy.

Sweet Onions   350°

2 lbs	onions thickly sliced	1 kg
2 tbsp	ketchup	30 mL
2 tbsp	water	30 mL
1 tbsp	liquid honey	15 mL
1 tbsp	milk-free margarine	15 mL
1/2 tsp	dry mustard	2 mL
	salt and pepper	

In saucepan of lightly salted water cook onions about 10 minutes. Drain and transfer to 6 cup (1.5 L) casserole dish. Mix together other ingredients and pour over onions. Bake for 1 hour at 350°F (180°C) or until onions are tender and glazed. Great with roasted or BBQ meat.

Salads and Sauces

Grilled/BBQ Potatoes

* amount depends on number of servings required

sliced potatoes - peeled or unpeeled - sliced
milk-free margarine - or olive oil
salt
pepper
onion - sliced
spice to taste
carrots (optional)

Tear off two double lengths of tin foil. You will require approximately 3 medium potatoes per piece. Grease with milk-free margarine or olive oil. Place sliced potatoes and carrots and onions—top with 2 tablespoons (30 mL) of margarine or oil. Spice to taste. Close tinfoil and wrap again with second piece. Place on hot BBQ on medium for approximately 1 hour.

Warm Potato Salad

4 cups	hot cooked potatoes - sliced or cubed	1 L
1/2 cup	chopped onion - fried in milk-free margarine	125 mL
1/2 cup	cooked ham or bacon	125 mL
1/2 cup	soy based mayonnaise	125 mL
	salt and pepper	

Combine all ingredients and serve hot.

Salads and Sauces

Macaroni Salad

1 cup	elbow macaroni or egg free noodle of choice	125 mL
6	slices of cooked bacon	6
	- fried crisp, save drippings	
2 tbsp	flour	30 mL
1/4 cup	vinegar	60 mL
1/3 cup	sugar	75 mL
1/8 tsp	salt	0.5 mL
	pepper	
1/2 cup	chopped celery	125 mL
4	sliced green onions	4

Cook elbow macaroni or egg free noodle of choice. Fry bacon until crisp, remove, let cool and crumble. Stir flour into bacon drippings. Add water and vinegar. Cook and stir until thickened. Stir in sugar, salt and pepper. Keep warm until macaroni is cooked. Add bacon, celery and onions to vinegar-sugar mixture. Heat until heated through. Pour over well drained macaroni. Stir—serve hot.

Coleslaw

3 cups	shredded cabbage	750 mL
1 cup	grated carrots	250 mL
1 cup	grated apple (optional)	250 mL
	small amount of grated onion	

Dressing

1/2–3/4 cup	soy based mayonnaise - milk and egg free	125–175 mL
4 tbsp	milk replacement	60 mL
2 tbsp	vinegar	30 mL
2 tbsp	sugar	30 mL
	salt and pepper	

Pour over salad and stir until well coated.

Salads and Sauces

Cabbage Salad

1	large head of cabbage - shredded	1
4	medium carrots - grated	4
1/2	medium onion - grated	1/2

Use a hand shredder or food processor to shred vegetables into large bowl.

Dressing

3/4 cup	white vinegar	175 mL
1/4 cup	salad oil	60 mL
1 cup	white sugar	250 mL
1 tbsp	salt	15 mL
	pepper	

Bring these ingredients to a boil, stirring constantly. Pour hot over vegetables. Stir to mix and press down on vegetables to cover well with brine. Store in covered container in fridge.

Raspberry Vinaigrette

1/4 cup	olive oil	60 mL
2 tbsp	white sugar	30 mL
2 tbsp	raspberry vinegar	30 mL
2 tbsp	sesame seeds (optional)	30 mL
	salt and pepper	

Pour over greens prior to serving.

* add raspberries or orange to greens.

Salads and Sauces

Guacamole

4	avocados	4
3 tbsp	salsa	45 mL
2 tsp	lemon juice	10 mL
	garlic salt and pepper to taste	

Mash together or use food processor. Make this just prior to serving.

chapter 10

Muffins

Muffins

Jam Filled Muffins   350°

2 2/3 cup	flour	650 mL
3 tsp	baking powder	15 mL
1 tsp	salt	5 mL
1/2 tsp	cinnamon	2 mL
2/3 cup	oil	150 mL
1 1/2 cups	white sugar	425 mL
1/4 cup	applesauce (1 egg)	60 mL
1 1/2 cups	milk replacement	375 mL
	strawberry jam or jam of choice	

Mix dry ingredients, slowly add liquids; do not over beat. Fill muffin cups 1/2 full, then add a tsp of jam. Cover with batter. Bake for 15–20 minutes at 350°F (180°C).

Topping

1/2–3/4 cup	melted milk-free margarine	125–175 mL
1 1/2 cups	white sugar	375 mL
2–3 tbsp	cinnamon (optional)	30–45 mL

Mix together sugar and cinnamon. Dip tops of muffins in melted margarine then into sugar/cinnamon mixture. Cool.

Crumb Topping

- for any muffins

1/2 cup	flour	125 mL
1/2 cup	sugar (white and brown mixed if you like)	125 mL
4 tbsp	milk-free margarine	60 mL

Rub together to make crumbs. Sprinkle on tops of muffins and gently press into dough.

Muffins

Breakfast Muffins — 350°

3 cups	bran cereal	750 mL
1 cup	boiling water	250 mL
2 1/2 cups	whole wheat flour or 1/2 white	625 mL
3/4 cup	sugar	175 mL
2 1/2 tsp	baking soda	12 mL
2 1/2 tsp	baking powder	12 mL
1 1/2 tsp	cinnamon	7 mL
1/2 tsp	salt	5 mL
3/4 cup	applesauce (or 2 eggs)	175 mL
2 cups	milk replacement	500 mL
1/2 cup	oil	125 mL
1/2–1 cup	raisins or dates	125–250 mL

Mix all dry ingredients together and add liquids. Do not over mix. Put into muffin cups and bake approximately 20 minutes at 350°F (180°C).

The Best Bran Muffins — 350°

These muffins are not only great tasting, they are also very forgiving when you add ingredients such as raisins, dates, cooked apples, bananas, or berries.

1 cup	oil	250 mL
2 cups	brown sugar	500 mL
1	can applesauce or cooked apples	1 mL
3 cups	brown flour	750 mL
1 1/2 cups	oatmeal	375 mL
1 1/2 cups	bran	375 mL
3 tsp	baking soda	15 mL
3 tsp	baking powder	15 mL
3 cups	milk replacement	750 mL

Stir together all dry ingredients, gently stir in liquids adding extra ingredients at the end. Put into muffin cups and bake for approximately 20 minutes at 350°F (180°C). These freeze well in an airtight container or bag.

Muffins

Blueberry Muffins 350°

2/3 cup	milk-free margarine	150 mL
1 3/4 cup	sugar	425 mL
1 1/2 tsp	vanilla	7 mL
2 3/4 cups	flour	675 mL
2 1/2 tsp	baking powder	12 mL
1/2 tsp	salt	2 mL
1 1/4 cup	milk replacement	310 mL
1 1/2 cups	frozen blueberries - add more if you like	375 mL
1/2 cup	applesauce/milk replacement (2 eggs)	125 mL

Cream together margarine, sugar, applesauce and vanilla. Add dry ingredients and milk replacement alternately. Gently stir in frozen blueberries and spoon into muffin cups. Bake for 15–20 minutes at 350°F (180°C).

This can be the base for many other ingredients other than blueberries—chocolate chips, other frozen fruit or left plain. Adding cake sprinkles can create the confetti look.

Sunny Morning Muffins 375°

2 cups	whole wheat flour	500 mL
1 cup	brown sugar	250 mL
2 tsp	baking powder	10 mL
1 tbsp	cinnamon	15 mL
2 cups	grated carrot	500 mL
1/3 cup	sunflower seeds - from nut free facility	75 mL
1	mashed banana or 3/4 cup (175 mL) cooked apple	1
1/2 cup	oil	125 mL
2 tsp	vanilla	10 mL
1/2 cup	applesauce/milk replacement (2 eggs beaten)	125 mL

Combine dry ingredients, stir in liquid ingredients and add carrots and banana. Spoon into muffin cups, bake for 15–20 minutes at 375°F (190°C).

Muffins

Muffins with Crumb Topping — 400°

3/4 cup	milk-free margarine	175 mL
2 cups	flour	500 mL
1 1/2 tsp	baking powder	7 mL
1 tsp	baking soda	5 mL
1/4 tsp	salt	1 mL
1 cup	sugar	250 mL
1 cup	milk replacement	250 mL
1/4 cup	applesauce/milk replacement (1 egg)	60 mL
1 tsp	vanilla	5 mL
1/2 cup	chocolate chips (or more)	125 mL

Combine together flour, baking powder, baking soda, sugar and margarine to make crumb mixture. Set aside 1/2 for topping. To the remainder add milk, vanilla and chocolate chips. Stir only until blended. Fill muffin cups 3/4 full and sprinkle with reserved crumbs on top. Bake for 15–20 minutes at 400°F (200°C).

Muffins

Healthy Muffins   375°

2 cups	whole wheat flour	500 mL
1 cup	toasted wheat germ	250 mL
2 tsp	baking powder	10 mL
1/2 tsp	baking soda	2 mL
2 tsp	cinnamon	10 mL
1 cup	mashed banana/cooked apple/zucchini or pumpkin	250 mL
1/3 cup	oil	75 mL
1 cup	milk replacement	250 mL
1/4 cup	applesauce/milk replacement (1 egg)	60 mL
1/4 cup	molasses	60 mL
1/4 cup	honey	60 mL
1/2 cup	raisins or cooked dates	125 mL

Combine all dry ingredients. Add liquids and gently stir. Add raisins or dates. Fill muffin cups and bake for 15–20 minutes at 375°F (190°C).

Chocolate Banana Muffins   350°

1/3 cup	oil	75 mL
1/2 cup	sugar	125 mL
1/4 cup	applesauce/milk replacement (1 egg)	60 mL
1 cup	mashed banana	250 mL
1 1/2 cups	chocolate chips - split into 2 portions	375 mL
1 cup	white or whole wheat flour	250 mL
2 tsp	baking powder	10 mL
1/2 tsp	salt	2 mL
1/2 tsp	cinnamon	2 mL

Combine dry ingredients. Stir together liquid ingredients including banana and 1 portion of chocolate chips. Combine dry and liquid mixtures together gently stirring. Spoon into muffin cups, sprinkle remaining portion of chocolate chips over tops of muffins. Bake 15–20 minutes at 350°F (180°C).

Muffins

Ginger Raisin Muffins   350°

2 cups	white or whole wheat flour	500 mL
1/4 tsp	baking soda	1 mL
1/2 tsp	ginger	2 mL
1/2 tsp	salt	2 mL
8 tbsp	melted milk-free margarine	120 mL
3 tsp	baking powder	15 mL
1/2 cup	milk replacement	125 mL
1/4 cup	applesauce (1 beaten egg)	60 mL
1/2 cup	molasses	125 mL
2/3 cup	washed raisins (or more)	150 mL

Canned pumpkin can be added to this recipe as well

1/4–1/2 cup	canned pumpkin	60–125 mL

Mix together all dry ingredients. Beat (egg if using) applesauce (pumpkin if using) and molasses. Slowly add this to the dry mixture. Add melted margarine. Fill muffin cups and bake 15–20 minutes at 350°F (180°C).

Banana Muffins   350°

3	large ripe bananas - mashed	3
3/4 cup	white sugar	175 mL
1/4 cup	applesauce (1 egg)	60 mL
1/3 cup	melted milk-free margarine	75 mL
1 tsp	baking soda	5 mL
1 tsp	baking powder	5 mL
1/2 tsp	salt	2 mL
1 1/2 cups	white or whole wheat flour	375 mL

Mix together dry ingredients. Mix together banana and all liquids. Stir together gently. Bake for 20–25 minutes at 350°F (180°C).

Muffins

Whole Wheat Pumpkin Muffins with Crumb Topping

350°

2 cups	whole wheat flour or 1/2 whole wheat and 1/2 white	500 mL
1 cup	raisins - well washed and dried	250 mL
1/3 cup	brown sugar	75 mL
1 1/2 tsp	baking powder	7 mL
1 tsp	baking soda	5 mL
1/2 tsp	salt	2 mL
1/2 tsp	cinnamon	2 mL
1/2 tsp	ginger	2 mL
1/4 cup	applesauce (1 egg)	60 mL
3/4 cup	pumpkin	175 mL
2 tbsp	grated orange rind (optional)	30 mL
1/2 cup	orange juice or milk replacement	125 mL
1/3 cup	oil	75 mL

Stir together dry ingredients and raisins. Add liquids and gently mix. Put into muffin cups and bake for 25 minutes at 350°F (180°C).

Topping (optional)

1/4 cup	white sugar	60 mL
1/4 cup	brown sugar	60 mL
1/4 cup	flour	60 mL
1/2 tsp	cinnamon	2 mL
1/4 cup	milk-free margarine	60 mL

Cut margarine into dry ingredients to form crumbly mixture. Sprinkle on tops of muffins and bake.

Muffins

Cherry/Apple Muffins   350°

1/2 cup	milk-free margarine melted	125 mL
2 1/2 cups	flour	625 mL
3/4 cup	sugar	175 mL
2 1/2 tsp	baking powder	12 mL
1/2 tsp	baking soda	2 mL
1/2 tsp	salt	2 mL
1	can cherry pie filling	1
1/4 cup	applesauce/milk replacement (1 egg)	60 mL
2	apples peeled, diced and cooked - can substitute applesauce crumb topping	2

Combine dry ingredients. Mix together liquids and stir into dry ingredients. Do not over mix. Fill muffin cups and top with crumb topping. Bake for 20–25 minutes at 350°F (180°C).

Orange Marmalade Muffins   350°

3/4 cup	marmalade	175 mL
1/2 cup	milk-free margarine	125 mL
1 cup	sugar	250 mL
1 1/2 cup	milk replacement	375 mL
1 tsp	salt	5 mL
1 3/4 cup	flour	425 mL
2 tsp	baking powder	10 mL
1/2 tsp	baking soda crumb topping (optional)	2 mL

Mix together all dry ingredients. Mix together all liquids and marmalade. Stir into dry ingredients. Put into muffin cups and top with crumb topping if you like. Bake at 350°F (180°C) for 15–20 minutes.

Instead of crumb topping, dip baked tops of muffins into melted margarine and then white sugar.

Muffins

Lemon Muffins 350°

1/3 cup	oil	75 mL
1/4 cup	sugar	60 mL
1/4 cup	applesauce or milk replacement (1 egg)	60 mL
1	6 oz (175 mL) can frozen lemonade or pink lemonade - thawed	1
2 1/2 tsp	baking powder	12 mL
1/2 tsp	salt	2 mL
1 1/2 cup	flour	375 mL
1/4 cup	milk replacement	60 mL

Mix together dry ingredients. Mix together liquid ingredients and gently stir into dry ingredients. Spoon into muffin cups and top with crumb topping if desired or dip into milk-free margarine, sugar and lemon juice once baked. Bake at 350°F (180°C) for 15–20 minutes.

Chocolate Chip Muffins 350°

1/3 cup	milk-free margarine - melted	75 mL
1/4 cup	applesauce/milk replacement (1 egg)	60 mL
1/2 cup	sugar	125 mL
1 1/2 cup	flour	375 mL
3 tsp	baking powder	15 mL
1/4 tsp	salt	1 mL
1 cup	safe chocolate chips	250 mL
1 cup	milk	250 mL

Mix dry ingredients, add chocolate chips. Combine liquids and stir into above until moistened. Bake for approximately 20–25 minutes at 350°F (180°C). Drizzle with melted chocolate chips when slightly cooled.

Muffins

Maple Muffins 350°

1/4 cup	milk-free margarine	60 mL
1/2 cup	white sugar	125 mL
1 tsp	salt	5 mL
1 1/4 cups	flour	310 mL
2 tsp	baking powder	10 mL
3/4 cup	rolled oats	175 mL
1/2 cup	milk replacement	125 mL
3/4 cup	maple syrup - increase if you like	175 mL

Glaze

1 tbsp	milk-free margarine	15 mL
1/2 cup	icing sugar	125 mL
2 tbsp	maple syrup	30 mL

Soften margarine, blend in sugar and salt. Add dry ingredients and blend with fork or pastry cutter until crumbly. Stir together milk and maple syrup, pour over dry ingredients and stir only to moisten. Fill muffin cups and bake for 20 minutes at 350°F (180°C). Glaze when slightly cooled.

Muffins

Strawberry Muffins 375°

2 cups	flour	500 mL
3/4 cup	sugar	175 mL
1 tsp	baking powder	5 mL
1/2 tsp	salt	2 mL
3/4-1 cup	milk replacement	175–250 mL
1/2 cup	oil	125 mL
1/4 cup	milk replacement or applesauce (or 1 egg)	60 mL
1 1/4 cups	chopped fresh strawberries	310 mL
	sugar for topping	
	melted milk-free margarine for topping	

Combine dry ingredients stir together gently. Stir together the liquids and add to the dry mixture. Stir together to moisten dough and add strawberries, do not over mix. Spoon into muffin cups and bake at 375°F (190°C) for approximately 15 minutes. When muffins are cooled dip the tops into melted margarine and then into sugar.

* Coloured sugar looks nice on these muffins

chapter 11

Extras

- *Managing Food Allergies*
- *Alternative names to look for in labels*
- *Resources*
- *Measurement Tables*

Managing Food Allergies

1. **Always have the required medication near the allergic person.** With young children, the medication should be in the keeping of the adult in charge, but always in the same location as the child. It cannot be of any help if it is in another location, for example left at the babysitter's house during the week. (We carried our son's medication in a separate small bag, not in my purse, until he was old enough to carry it with him in a backpack. His medication is inside a Medic Alert® bag, which is easy to identify. Inside the bag are our phone numbers and a copy of his Medic Alert® information.)

2. **Always wear medical identification**—Medic Alert® identification alerts medical personnel and others to vital medical information. This allows medical personnel or anyone else to identify the problem quickly and give proper care.

3. Never hesitate to inform those around you of the allergies you or your child have. The more informed others are, the more co-operation you can expect.

4. Particularly when dealing with children, be certain that caregivers, coaches, in fact anyone who may be in charge other than you, are well informed of the allergies, symptoms and what to do. Type a clear description of what to do in case of a reaction, including specific symptoms and emergency contact numbers. This can be left with caregivers, coaches and teachers. Always be available via a cell phone or other phone contact—in case a reaction does occur, you can give instructions over the phone. Stay with your child in a new situation until you feel confident that things can be managed.

5. Carry an EpiPen® Trainer with you or with a child's medication. This training tool assists in explaining the situation and allows for hands-on training. Encourage your child to participate in training others when he or she is of an age to do so. This not only gives practice but also encourages independence and confidence.

6. While many fast food chains have very detailed ingredient listings, be aware that these can change from country to country or at any time, so always review them.

7. Always call the manufacturer if you have a question about a product. Most are very prepared to answer questions regarding food allergies.

8. Be proactive with respect to allergic children. For example, when they are in school, speak with the health nurse who will be training the staff. Co-operate with these efforts and become involved, possibly by doing a presentation. Schools should have a well-coordinated management plan in place. A coordinated plan could save a life. Know the protocol, and teach it to your child.

9. When purchasing pet food and treats, be aware of ingredients—milk, egg and peanuts are very common. If the residue remains on the pet's fur or mouth and comes in contact with the allergic person, a reaction can occur.

Managing Food Allergies

10. Do not eat previously-cut-up vegetables, fruit or meat unless you can be certain that the knife, cutting board and counter were allergen-free. Do not use previously-opened margarine, jams, jellies or spreads, as they could have been contaminated by allergens on utensils.

11. Always check new medications for ingredients. Tell all health personnel—doctor, dentist, health nurse, and pharmacist—prior to any treatment.

12. Check all cosmetics, lotions, and personal products prior to use not only by the allergic person, but also by those in contact with him or her. Often you have to call the manufacturer directly, as ingredients are not always listed on packaging. Most companies are very helpful in these situations; many even have emergency response information after regular business hours.

13. Ingredients can change at any time—always check the ingredients on store-bought items and at restaurants.

14. When using foods someone in the home is allergic to, be sure to dispose of dishcloths, towels, and anything else that could have come in contact with the allergen. Wash counters or tables with a clean dishcloth. Wash any utensils diligently (we wash them and then put through the dishwasher, and we also have some separate utensils that are not used for anything but cooking with milk or eggs.)

15. Always inform staff of allergies when making plane, train or bus reservations. Efforts will be made to accommodate special needs.

16. Always be prepared with allergen free snacks/treats on hand. This can help when others are offered a treat. Examples would include having special allergen-free frozen treats in the summer, having a labelled bag of treats at school for those surprise treat days, and having a small treat ready for unexpected events.

17. Always check with your children, especially when they are getting older, how they would like different situations handled with respect to their special needs.

18. Keep the lines of communication open with children and teens. As children mature, the issues surrounding their allergies change. They need support to continue with their independence and with management of their particular allergies.

19. Regularly review symptoms and procedures in case of a reaction. Regular reviews with your allergist are also important.

20. Be aware of expiry dates on EpiPen®, and re-order as required.

Managing Food Allergies

21. When invited to a party or event, some suggestions are as follows:

    a) Speak with the host/hostess to find out the menu and where the meal will be served—restaurant, catered or in the home.

    b) If you can, replicate what is being served, free of allergens. Keep this away from the main meal, and well labelled. For example. at a child's birthday party, check the menu with host/hostess—e.g. hot dogs, potato chips, candy, and chocolate cake with white frosting. Inform the host/hostess about the child's allergies and request that treats such as nuts and peanuts not be served. Determine if the foods being served are free of allergens. If not, bring safe food. Supervise/assist with cooking so food does not get mixed up. Check candy labels and replace what you need to. Put safe potato chips in a bowl for your child so there will not be any cross-contamination between flavours. In most cases cakes will not be safe, so make a cake to look similar and bring 2–3 pieces, well labelled, for when it is time to serve cake. If other guests are informed ahead of time about the child's allergies and the possible consequences, they are more likely to co-operate and be more understanding when asked, for example, to wash after eating foods containing allergens. This is a very simple meal plan, but shows how planning ahead can provide for fun and safety.

    c) Ask to stay and assist with food preparation and snacks. This helps to prevent cross-contamination. Most hosts and hostesses appreciate the help, and are grateful for not being left with the responsibility to manage alone.

    d) In the case of a catered meal, speak with the catering coordinator to check the menu. This person will often put you in touch with the chef in charge of the meal. He/she may be able to provide a meal free of allergens yet similar to the catered meal, or may suggest that you bring your own and they can heat it for you. (We have done both and had positive experiences. Of course, if it is a close family function you have a little more ability to put forth suggestions such as no peanuts/nuts present.) Always review this with the caterers close to the date. On the day of the function you have to play an active role—the co-ordination and safety can not be left completely up to others. Successful catered meals are always co-operative efforts. Be reasonable and do not have expectations that are not attainable.

Managing Food Allergies

e) In the case of restaurant meals, try to plan ahead and speak with the restaurant manager, chef or cooks prior to going to the establishment. Try to do this during a time that is not busy for the restaurant; this both respects their time and allows them to assist you fully. If you cannot pre-plan prior to going, try to show up when the restaurant is not busy, so you can speak with the appropriate staff. Be reasonable about choices. (For example, for Aaron we would check the fries and possibly a hamburger, and avoid breaded chicken breast and soup as these are more likely to be made with eggs and milk. I have been taken by staff into many kitchens to check ingredients personally. Most restaurant personnel have been extremely helpful; on several occasions staff have suggested that they make something fresh and free of allergens.)

22. Accommodating food allergies when travelling can be a challenge. The following are some tips to make travelling easier:

a) Try to stay in properties or hotels that offer kitchen facilities. This allows you to enjoy your holiday *and* eat safely.

b) For short stays, or where kitchen facilities are not available, always request a refrigerator for your room. This allows you to bring some food that is safe. If possible, plan ahead and tell the management about the food allergies. Often, arrangements can be made with the restaurant chef to accommodate special diet requests.

c) Travelling in a motor home allows for "food freedom" as well. (We have found this a great way to take longer trips.)

Alternative names to look for in labels

Egg

- albumin
- ovomucoid
- globulin
- livetin
- ovalbumin
- lysozyme
- apovitellanin
- phosvitin

Milk

- whey
- sodium caseinate
- lactoglobulin
- lactose
- casein
- lactalbumin
- curds

Nuts/peanut

- arachis oil
- anacardium nuts
- ground nuts
- marzipan
- goober nuts
- mandelonas

Resources

Resources for reliable information on food allergies

- Anaphylaxis Canada
  416 Moore Avenue, Ste 306
  Toronto ON M4G 1C9
  Canada
  Telephone: 416.785.5666
  Web site: www.gosafe.ca

- Medic Alert® International
  The most trusted name in emergency medical information services
  Telephone: 1.800.432.5378
  Web site: www.medicalert.org

- The Food Allergy
  and Anaphylaxis Network
  11781 Lee Jackson Highway, Ste 160
  Fairfax VA 22033-3309
  USA
  Toll free: 1.800.929.4040
  Web site: www.foodallergy.org

- Canadian Food Inspection Agency
  Web site: www.inspection.gc.ca
  **Registration is available for up to date recalls due to undeclared allergens

- The Lung Association
  Web site: www.lung.ca
  Telephone: 1.888.566.5864

- Allerex
  P.O. Box 13307
  Kanata ON K2K 1X5
  Canada
  Telephone: 613.831.7733
  Web site: www.allerex.ca

- Canadian Pediatric Society
  Web site: www.caringforkids.cps.ca/eating/FoodAllergies.htm

- Allergy/Asthma Information Association
  Registered head office
  P.O. Box 100
  Toronto ON M9W 5K9
  Canada
  Telephone: 416.679.9521
  Toll free: 1.800.611.7011
  Web site: www.aaia.ca

- Canadian Restaurant
  and Food Services Association
  Web site: www.crfa.ca

Measurement Tables

Throughout this book measurements are given in Conventional and Metric measure. To compensate for differences between the two measurements due to rounding, a full metric measure is not always used. An exact metric conversion is given below as well as working equivalent (Metric Standard Measure).

Oven Temperatures

250°F	120°C
275°F	140°C
300°F	150°C
325°F	160°C
350°F	180°C
375°F	190°C
400°F	200°C
425°F	220°C
450°F	230°C
475°F	250°C
500°F	260°C
500°F	260°C
525°F	270°C

Length

1 inch	2.5 centimetres

Pans

8"x8"	20x20 cm
9"x9"	22x22 cm
9"x13"	22x33 cm
10"x15"	25x38 cm
11"x17"	28x43 cm
8"x2" round	20x5 cm
9"x2" round	22x5 cm
10"x4.5" tube	25x11 cm
8"x4"x3" loaf	20x10x7.5 cm
9"x5"x3" loaf	22x12.5x7.5 cm

Weight

1	ounce	30	grams
1/2	pound	250	grams
3/4	pound	375	grams
1	pound	500	grams
1 1/2	pounds	750	grams
2	pounds	1	kilogram
3	pounds	1.5	kilograms
4	pounds	2	kilograms
5	pounds	2.5	kilograms

Measurement Tables

Conventional Measure	Metric Exact Conversion Millilitre (mL)	Metric Standard Measure Millilitre (mL)

Spoons

1/8 teaspoon (tsp)	0.6 mL	0.5 mL
1/4 teaspoon (tsp)	1.2 mL	1 mL
1/2 teaspoon (tsp)	2.4 mL	2 mL
1 teaspoon (tsp)	4.7 mL	5 mL
2 teaspoons (tsp)	9.4 mL	10 mL
1 tablespoon (Tbsp)	14.2 mL	15 mL

Cups

1/4 cup (4 Tbsp)	56.8 mL	60 mL
1/3 cup (5 1/3 Tbsp)	75.6 mL	75 mL
1/2 cup (8 Tbsp)	113.7 mL	125 mL
2/3 cup (10 2/3 Tbsp)	151.2 mL	150 mL
3/4 cup (12 Tbsp)	170.5 mL	175 mL
1 cup (16 Tbsp)	227.3 mL	250 mL
4 1/2 cups	1022.9 mL	1000 mL (1 L)

Dry Measurements

1 oz	28.3 g	28 g
2 oz	56.7 g	57 g
3 oz	85.0 g	85 g
4 oz	113.4 g	125 g
5 oz	141.7 g	140 g
6 oz	170.1 g	170 g
7 oz	198.4 g	200 g
8 oz	226.8 g	250 g
16 oz	453.6 g	500 g
32 oz	907.2 g	1000 g (1 kg)

Index

A
Antipasto 129
Apple Crisp with Marshmallows 48
Apple Oatmeal Cookies 43
Applesauce Raisin Cake 26

B
Bacon Wrapped Pork Roast 107
Baked Vegetables 140
Bakery Shop Icing 69
Banana Muffins 151
Bannock 13
Basic White Sauce 130
BBQ Beef in a Slow Cooker 99
BBQ Potatoes 138
BBQ Spareribs 103
Bean Salad 134
Bean Soup 120
Beet/Cabbage Borscht 125
Berry Crisp 62
Berry Glaze for Cake 74
Biscuits - Grandma's 13
Blueberry Muffins 148
Blueberry Oatmeal Bread 16
Blueberry Tea Ring 54
Blueberry/Fruit Crumb Cake 56
Boiled Icing 70
Breakfast Muffins 147
Brownies 27

C
Cabbage Salad 143
Candy Apples 82
Candy Cookies 38
Caramel Corn 76
Caramel Dumplings 52
Caramel Fried Ice Cream 84
Caramel Icing 69
Caramel Sandwich Cookies 32
Carrot and Raisin Salad 131
Carrot Cake 30
Cereal and Pretzel Snack 83
Cherry/Apple Muffins 153
Chicken and Noodles 111
Chicken Fingers 111
Chicken Noodle Soup 123
Chicken or Turkey Marinara 114
Chicken or Turkey Tacos 113
Chili 91
Chocolate Banana Muffins 150
Chocolate Cake 24
Chocolate Cake Cookies 34
Chocolate Cherry Crunchie 53
Chocolate Chip Muffins 154
Chocolate Chip/Oatmeal Cookies 33
Chocolate Icing 72
Chocolate Pinwheel Cookies 32
Chocolate Pretzels 85
Chocolate Pudding Cake 29
Chocolate Syrup 86
Christmas Pudding 59
Cinnamon Twists 42
Coffee Whipped Topping Frosting 71
Coleslaw 142
Coloured Popcorn Balls 77
Cooked Icing 68
Cookie Monsters 43
Corn Chowder 121
Cornbread 21
Cornish Hens with Wild Rice 117
Cream of Carrot Soup 126
Cream of Chicken Soup 123
Cream of Potato 121
Cream of Tomato Soup 125
Crumb Cake 27
Crumb Topping 146
Crunchy Coated Potatoes 139
Curry Chicken with Coconut 116

D
Dijon Sauce 112
Dill Cucumbers 133
Double Chocolate Chip Cookies 46
Doughnuts 20

F
Fancy Potatoes 137
Favourite Salad 135
Filling for Cinnamon buns 22
Flour Tortillas 21
French Toast 14
Fresh Raspberry Cake 28
Fried Pepper and Beans 132
Frozen Dessert Squares 61
Frozen Treats 80
Fruit Sherbet 83
Fruit Square 63
Fudge 78
Fudge Icing 73
Fudge Sundae Pie 51

Index

G
Garlic Bread 12
Garlic Chicken 110
Ginger Chicken/Turkey Kabobs 110
Ginger Raisin Muffins 151
Ginger Snaps 35
Gingerbread (old fashioned) 34
Graham Wafer Cake 25
Graham Wafer Crumbs 78
Greek Lemon Potatoes 136
Grilled/BBQ Potatoes 141
Guacamole 144
Gumdrop Raisin Cookies 36

H
Hamburger & Chips Casserole 96
Hamburger Soup 122
Hawaiian Style Spareribs 106
Healthy Muffins 150
Healthy Snack Cookies 39
Honey Curry Chicken 112
Hot Chocolate 87
Hot Fudge Sauce 87
Hot Wings 108

I
Icing for Cut-out Cookies 70

J
Jam Filled Muffins 146

L
Layered Casserole 96
Lefse 14
Lemon Muffins 154

M
Macaroni Salad 142
Maple Cream Fudge 79
Maple Muffins 155
Marinated Beef 100
Marinated Steak 98
Marshmallow Frosting 73
Marshmallow Popcorn Balls 77
Marshmallow Shapes 81
Matrimonial Cake (Date Cake) 28
Meat & Rice Cabbage Rolls 95
Meat Loaf 93
Meat Loaf 92
Milk-Free Biscuits 22
Minestrone Soup 124
Mocha Fudge Brownie Icing 71
Mocha Fudge Brownies with Icing 64
Muffins with Crumb Topping 149

N
No-Bake Chocolate Cookies 42

O
Oatcakes 15
Oatmeal Bread 12
Oatmeal Cookies 40
Oatmeal Date Cookies 44
Old Fashioned Sugar Cookies 41
Old Fashioned Fudge 86
Onions for the BBQ 135
Orange Marmalade Muffins 153
Oven Fried Chicken 118
Oven Fried Rice 118
Oven Potatoes 139

P
Pancakes/waffles 20
Pasta Sauces - cream 130
Pea Soup 120
Peanut Butter FREE Cookies 45
Pepper Steak 99
Pie Dough with Shortening 52
Popcorn Balls 76
Popsicles 88
Pork Cutlets 102
Pork Kabobs 105
Puffed Wheat Cake 25
Pumpkin Dessert 49

Q
Quick and Easy Potatoes 137
Quick Cinnamon Rolls 19

R
Raisin Pie Filling 55
Raspberry Vinaigrette 143
Resources for reliable information
    on food allergies 163
Rhubarb Bavarian Dessert 57
Rhubarb Crunch 58
Rice Crispy Cake 24
Ribs with Hot Sauce 107
Rice Salad 133
Roast Pork with Garlic and Rosemary . . . 106
Rolled Ginger Cookies (soft) 35

Index

Rolled Steak 101
Rum Sauce for Christmas Pudding 60

S

Salsa 128
Sauce for Pork or Chicken 104
Sausage Casserole 104
Scalloped Potatoes 136
Scones 15
Scottish Oat Scones 17
Shortbread Tart Shells 50
Smothered Chicken 109
Soda Bread 17
Soup Broth - Beef Stock 122
Spaghetti and Meatballs 94
Spicy Broiled Chicken 115
Spicy Chicken Wings 108
Steak Strips on Pasta or Rice 100
Stew 97
Strawberry Dessert 50
Strawberry Muffins 156
Stuffing for Chicken or Turkey 117
Sunny Morning Muffins 148
Supreme Salad 131
Sweet and Sour Chicken 115
Sweet and Sour Meat Balls 93
Sweet Apple Turnover 55
Sweet Onions 140
Sweet Potato Casserole 132

T

Tacos 90
Tapioca Pudding 66
Tea Biscuits 18
The Best Bran Muffins 147
The Best Icing 72
Topping for any Fruit Crisp 65
Trifle 65
Turkey or Chicken Burgers 113

U

Unbaked Coconut Slice 61

V

Variation of Tart Shells 51
Vegetable Salad 138

W

Warm Potato Salad 141
Whipped Shortbread 41
White Bread 10
White Cake 26
White Cut-out Cookies 37
White Hard Sauce for Christmas Pudding . . . 60
White Icing 68
Whole Wheat bread 11
Whole Wheat Pumpkin Muffins
   with Crumb Topping 152

ISBN 1-41203873-1

Made in the USA